Creating, Grading, and Using Virtual Assessments

This book provides a variety of strategies for creating, grading, and using assessments in the virtual setting.

With more teaching and learning taking place online, teachers are adjusting their strategies for creating, grading, and using virtual assessments. This strategies-based book helps you understand the key challenges and solutions to delivering virtual assessments, including use of quizzes, digital worksheets, grading, preventing cheating, and considerations of equity, quality, choice, and efficiency. Designed so that you can pick it up and start reading from any chapter, this book covers topics such as:

- how to create, grade, and use traditional forms of assessment in the virtual space;
- how to leverage discussion for meaningful learning in the virtual classroom;
- how to create, grade, and use virtual performances and projects;
- digital tools that may be helpful in engaging with and assessing students in the virtual environment.

Based on research and full of practical examples, this book guides educators, professional learning teams, and whole schools in implementing a successful virtual assessment plan for all types of intended learning objectives.

Kate Wolfe Maxlow is Director of Innovation and Professional Learning for Hampton City Schools, Virginia, and an adjunct professor for Old Dominion University, USA.

Karen L. Sanzo is Professor in the Darden College of Education and Professional Studies at Old Dominion University, USA.

James R. Maxlow has been a public school teacher and administrator for over 20 years with a doctorate in Curriculum and Educational Technology. He is currently the Technology Support Manager for Hampton City Schools, Virginia.

Other Eye On Education Books Available From Routledge
(www.routledge.com/eyeoneducation)

**Strategies for Developing and Supporting School Leaders:
Stepping Stones to Great Leadership**
Karen L. Sanzo

**20 Formative Assessment Strategies that Work:
A Guide Across Content and Grade Levels**
Kate Wolfe Maxlow and Karen L. Sanzo

**Leadership for Deeper Learning: Facilitating
School Innovation and Transformation**
Jayson Richardson, Justin Bathon, and Scott McLeod

**A Practical Guide to Leading Green Schools: Partnering
with Nature to Create Vibrant, Fourishing, Sustainable Schools**
Cynthia L. Uline and Lisa A. W. Kensler

**Rural America's Pathways to College and Career:
Steps for Student Success and School Improvement**
Rick Dalton

Bringing Innovative Practices to Your School: Lessons from International Schools
Jayson W. Richardson

A Guide to Impactful Teacher Evaluations: Let's Finally Get It Right!
Joseph O. Rodgers

**A Guide to Early College and Dual Enrollment Programs:
Designing and Implementing Programs for Student Achievement**
Russ Olwell

The Strategy Playbook for Educational Leaders: Principles and Processes
Isobel Stevenson and Jennie Weiner

Unpacking Your learning Targets: Aligning Student Learning to Standards
Sean McWherter

Strategic Talent Leadership for Educators: A Practical Toolkit
Amy A. Holcombe

Becoming a Transformative Leader: A Guide to Creating Equitable Schools
Carolyn M. Shields

**Working with Students that Have Anxiety:
Creative Connections and Practical Strategies**
Beverley H. Johns, Donalyn Heise, Adrienne D. Hunter

Implicit Bias in Schools: A Practitioner's Guide
Gina Laura Gullo, Kelly Capatosto, and Cheryl Staats

Creating, Grading, and Using Virtual Assessments

Strategies for Success in the
K-12 Classroom

Kate Wolfe Maxlow, Karen L. Sanzo,
and James R. Maxlow

NEW YORK AND LONDON

First published 2022
by Routledge
605 Third Avenue, New York, NY 10158

and by Routledge
2 Park Square, Milton Park, Abingdon, Oxon, OX14 4RN

Routledge is an imprint of the Taylor & Francis Group, an informa business

© 2022 Taylor & Francis

The right of Kate Wolfe Maxlow, Karen L. Sanzo, and James R. Maxlow to be identified as authors of this work has been asserted by them in accordance with sections 77 and 78 of the Copyright, Designs and Patents Act 1988.

All rights reserved. No part of this book may be reprinted or reproduced or utilised in any form or by any electronic, mechanical, or other means, now known or hereafter invented, including photocopying and recording, or in any information storage or retrieval system, without permission in writing from the publishers.

Trademark notice: Product or corporate names may be trademarks or registered trademarks, and are used only for identification and explanation without intent to infringe.

Library of Congress Cataloging-in-Publication Data
Names: Maxlow, Kate Wolfe, author. | Sanzo, Karen, author. | Maxlow, James Richard, author.
Title: Creating, grading, and using virtual assessments : strategies for success in the K-12 classroom / Kate Wolfe Maxlow, Karen L. Sanzo, James Maxlow.
Description: 1 Edition. | New York : Routledge, 2022. | Includes bibliographical references.
Identifiers: LCCN 2021020424 (print) | LCCN 2021020425 (ebook) | ISBN 9781032056982 (Hardback) | ISBN 9781032059723 (Paperback) | ISBN 9781003200093 (eBook)
Subjects: LCSH: Educational evaluation—Methodology. | Curriculum-based assessment. | Computer managed instruction. | Internet in education. | Educational technology.
Classification: LCC LB2822.75 .M387 2022 (print) | LCC LB2822.75 (ebook) | DDC 379.1/58—dc23
LC record available at https://lccn.loc.gov/2021020424
LC ebook record available at https://lccn.loc.gov/2021020425

ISBN: 978-1-032-05698-2 (hbk)
ISBN: 978-1-032-05972-3 (pbk)
ISBN: 978-1-003-20009-3 (ebk)

DOI: 10.4324/9781003200093

Typeset in Optima
by KnowledgeWorks Global Ltd.

Access the Support Material: www.routledge.com/9781032059723

Contents

About the Authors viii
Preface x

1. **Creating, Grading, and Using Traditional Assessment Strategies** 1
2. **Creating, Grading, and Using Classwork and Homework** 25
3. **Virtual Discussion Strategies** 62
4. **Virtual Performance Strategies** 94
5. **Virtual Projects** 122

About the Authors

Dr. Kate Wolfe Maxlow started her career teaching third and fourth grade before working as an instructional coach, an educational consultant, and a professional learning coordinator. She is currently the Director of Innovation and Professional Learning for Hampton City Schools, Virginia, and moonlights as a virtual teacher for upper elementary and middle school students with a focus on creating online role-playing adventure games for literature and history. She also works as an adjunct professor for Old Dominion University, and has taught online at every level from preK through graduate school. She lives in Williamsburg, Virginia, with her husband James, their two wonderful children, and their crazy, giant Great Pyrenees/Poodle dog, Barkley.

Dr. Karen L. Sanzo is a Professor in the Darden College of Education and Professional Studies at Old Dominion University. She began her career in education as a middle school mathematics teacher, later serving as an elementary school administrator. She has taught in the virtual learning space for over 20 years. Her work centers around the areas of organizational innovation, continuous improvement, and leadership preparation and development. She frequently works with K-12 districts to support their work in the areas of formative assessment and innovation and has also served as Principal Investigator for several national and state-level grants around the areas of school leadership, formative assessment, STEM education, and the K-12/higher education cybersecurity pipeline. Outside of work, she enjoys taking trips to the beach with her family and running lots of miles in ultramarathon events.

Dr. James R. Maxlow maintains a passion for continuously improving public education—a passion that began when he first entered college and continues to this day. While earning degrees in Mathematics and Computer

Science from Christopher Newport University, and most recently a doctorate in Curriculum and Educational Technology from the College of William and Mary, James has put his knowledge and skills to use as a public school teacher and administrator, dedicating 21 years to his craft. James' particular areas of interest include leveraging instructional technologies and coaching strategies to improve the effectiveness of classroom teachers, as well as exploring the curricular integration of technology resources such as educational gaming and electronic collaboration between students. He has authored multiple articles in ISTE's *Learning and Leading* magazine and recently published an academic study on the use of the *Mission US* educational game in a middle school social studies program.

Preface
How to Use This Book

Welcome!

The way we understand education—how to teach, assess, and engage students—has demonstrably and irrevocably changed since March, 2020. If you're reading this book then you, like us, have been working in myriad ways to reimagine our work with students. There are many facets to crafting a high-quality virtual learning environment, including instructional design and delivery, assessment of learning, developing learning communities of practice, working with parents and other stakeholders, along with other aspects of school. In this book, we focus on assessment of learning in the virtual setting. Our main purpose is to provide a variety of strategies for creating, grading, and using virtual assessments and their results in the virtual setting. While many of the considerations for virtual assessments are the same as in-person assessments, assessing virtually presents some different challenges and opportunities of which we need to be cognizant. We appreciate you taking the virtual assessment journey with us in this book.

Who Should Use This Book

Our book is designed to provide practical, immediately implementable assessment strategies for teachers, instructional leaders, and administrators. Individual educators can pick up this text and easily apply the strategies provided. Further, professional learning teams and whole schools can use the text as a book study. We have provided suggested professional development templates for use at the end of each chapter.

We also find this text is quite helpful for those working in the field of higher education and supporting the development of aspiring and current teachers and administrators. The strategies being offered in the text are ones that can be explored for their students to use in their own PK-12 work. Additionally, while not geared towards teaching in higher education, the same principles are applicable for those teaching at the undergraduate and graduate levels.

Features of This Book

We have designed this book so that you can pick it up and start reading from any chapter. It isn't necessary to read it straight through and you are encouraged to start where you feel would be most beneficial for you in your work and makes the most sense for you at the time. We begin with discussing how to create, grade, and use traditional forms of assessment in the virtual space. From there, we explore classwork and homework with particular attention to how today's learners are truly different from Pk-12 students in the past and how to ensure we are engaging students in the virtual space. Expanding on the topic of engagement, Chapter 3 looks at how to leverage discussion for meaningful learning in the virtual classroom. From there, we then speak to how to create, grade, and use virtual performances in Chapter 4 and virtual projects in Chapter 5.

Because examples matter, we have also created case studies near the end of each chapter. The case studies follow the Identify—Plan—Apply—Assess—Refine format developed by Sanzo, Myran, and Caggiano (2014) in Formative Assessment Leadership. The framework can help both the individual educator, as well as professional learning teams, meaningfully go through the various assessment stages in order to ensure all students' needs are being met and, where needed, instructional and assessment adjustments are made. Additionally, we provide an example at the end of each chapter how you can work with your learning team or school to use this book in a professional development activity.

We also provide the names of specific digital tools that, at the time of publication, we have found to be quite helpful in engaging with and assessing students in the virtual environment. However, we recognize that digital tools are constantly changing and evolving and that by the time you read this book there may be other tools available that can better assist you in your work. Therefore, it is essential that you use your own professional judgment in selecting these tools, as well as more broadly in deciding which concepts in this text you want to try out and apply in the classroom.

Online Resources

Lastly, we invite you to take the time to check out some of our online resources at www.routledge.com/9781032059723. We have taken several of the planning and grading tools from this book and converted them to individual documents so that you can download and edit them for your personal use. These include tools such as the I Do/We Do/You Do planning template for homework and classwork, the scrum chart for project-based learning, the single-point rubric for assessing performances, and many more. While we give examples of how to use these various tools in the book itself, we believe in the importance of educators making changes to ensure that tools fit the needs of their students, and hope that you will find these tools helpful for your virtual classroom.

Reference

Sanzo, K. L., Myran, S., & Caggiano, J. (2014). *Formative assessment leadership: Identify, plan, apply, assess, refine*. Routledge.

Creating, Grading, and Using Traditional Assessment Strategies

One of the questions we are frequently asked is, "How can I make sure that my students don't cheat when doing their online assessments?" The reality is that due to the nature of virtual assessments, there are simply more opportunities for students to gain answers from places other than their own brains. Even if the students take an assessment synchronously with their cameras on, the teacher has a limited view of the area around the student. Students can have a second device in their lap or even a family member whispering answers off to the side. That being said, the first question should not be, "How can we keep students from cheating?" as much as, "What is the point of this assessment?" The reason that we use a particular assessment type will inform how we can assure the results are as valid and reliable as possible for our intended purposes.

Overview of Traditional Assessments

Before we can understand how to create, grade, and use traditional assessments, we must first define what is meant by these terms. It is also crucial to understand when to use traditional assessments, as well as their strengths and limitations in terms of providing information about student learning. Frequently, we see that teachers' default way of thinking is that traditional assessments are the best way to assess students' learning, but the truth is that there are both pros and cons when using this type of assessment. Moreover, because it is much more challenging to regulate the sources students can access while being virtually assessed, teachers will have to think very carefully about whether to use this type of assessment, and if it is used, how to implement it in the best way possible.

Defining Traditional Assessments

The reason we chose traditional assessments to be the first assessment strategy is because these assessments tend to be thought as the "default" assessment strategy. When most people reflect upon their schooling and consider "assessments," they usually think of tests and quizzes that are composed of multiple-choice, true/false, matching, fill-in-the-blank, and short-answer items. Most likely they remember being told to keep their eyes on their own papers or computer screens, having to supply all information from memory, and anxiously awaiting a score on their work that could dramatically impact their overall course grade.

> It is crucial to understand when to use traditional assessments

Generally, traditional assessments are a *formal* type of assessment, in that the teacher prepares them in advance and they are completely separate from instruction. There tend to be two major categories of traditional assessment items: select-response and supply-response (also called "constructed response"). *Select-response items* require students to choose the correct answer(s) from choices supplied by the test-creator. Examples include multiple-choice, multiple-select, and matching items. Note that the multiple-choice category also includes true or false items; the term "multiple choice" only requires that more than one choice is provided for students. Multiple-select items are similar, except they may have more than one correct answer and students have to select *all* answers that correctly answer or complete the item stem. Matching items generally supply students with two columns of information, and students are required to correctly match information on the left-hand side with information on the right-hand side. Frequently, these types of items are used to assess whether students can accurately pair basic terms, events, or

> There tend to be two major categories of traditional assessment items: select-response and supply-response

people with the appropriate provided descriptions. The benefits of select-response items for teachers are that they are typically easy and quick to grade, they can assess wide swaths of information at a time, and they are considered to have "objective" (i.e., right or wrong) answers. Individual items are also relatively quick for students to complete, although, of course, an abundance of any item type will make an assessment take longer. The downside of these types of items, however, is that students can guess answers, which may lead to a misdiagnosis of what students know and can do. Furthermore, these types of items generally cannot assess higher-level cognitive skills, such as students' abilities to evaluate information or create new products or processes.

Supply-response items, on the other hand, require students to generate their own answers. Answers can be as short as a single punctuation mark, number, or word, or as long as an essay (though frequently, essays that are part of a traditional assessment are shorter than standalone essays; a general rule of thumb is that essays for traditional assessments are two to five paragraphs long). Items included in the supply-response category can include fill-in-the-blank, labeling diagrams, filling in graphic organizers, short answer (generally one to five sentences). One strength of supply-response items is that while students can still make guesses, there is a decreased chance that they will be able to correctly guess the answer without having at least a modicum of understanding. These items are also useful for assessing higher-level cognitive skills, such as students' abilities to use information to analyze, evaluate, and even create. (That being said, evaluating students' ability to create is often better done through assessments such as projects.) The most frequently cited drawbacks of these types of assessment items, however, are that they take longer for students to answer and for teachers to grade. Depending on the complexity of the questions, judging the quality of the answers may also be subjective. Requiring subjective judgment is not an inherently bad characteristic (this will be discussed more in later chapters), but it does require more thought and justification on the part on the part of the teacher.

> Select-response items generally cannot assess higher-level cognitive skills

When to Use Traditional Assessments

One of the overall benefits of traditional assessments is that they can usually be completed by students in a single sitting. Even when they include supply-response

> Traditional assessments frequently require a teacher to unpack the intended learning objectives

items, they are generally considered to be more objective overall than assessments such as projects and discussions. They tend to be faster for teachers to grade and do not require multiple rounds of feedback and revisions. We, therefore, recommend that teachers employ traditional assessments when they want or need to assess students' understanding of *basic* knowledge and application. This will frequently require a teacher to unpack the intended learning objectives before beginning a unit to determine *which* knowledge and skills from the unit can be assessed using traditional methods and which need a different type of assessment to get an accurate picture of student learning.

Creating Traditional Assessments

How we choose to create virtual traditional assessments will depend on how we intend to use them. Choosing and using the appropriate virtual tools is dependent on whether the major purpose of the assessment is to provide *summative* information (i.e., to make a judgment about student mastery at a predetermined point in time to provide information to students and families), or *formative* information (i.e., provide both the teacher and the student with information about current student understanding with the main purpose of informing future teaching and learning strategies). As noted in the introduction, it is possible to use an assessment for both formative and summative purposes, but to determine *how* to create the assessment, teachers must first determine the *main* purpose.

While we should always consider issues of validity and reliability when creating any assessment, these concepts become crucial when designing traditional assessments. They are even more critical for *virtual* traditional assessments because teachers do not have the same ability as they do in-person to regulate how students complete the assessments. Nevertheless, some strategies can be used to increase the level to which we can be sure that the assessment is providing valid inferences about students' understanding.

Comparison Versus Mastery Purposes

While there may be other purposes for assessments, two main purposes, often at odds with one another, are to assess student mastery versus to compare students to a predetermined "acceptable" measure or to their peers. When we use assessments to compare students, all students take the test at the same time, generally with few or no chances to improve their score once they complete the assessment and it has been graded. An assessment that compares student scores to how they should perform at a given time is called a *criterion-referenced assessment*. State-created standardized assessments and other diagnostic assessments usually fall into this category. Results may be categorized as "passing" or "advanced" or "below grade level" (though obviously there are several other possible designations). Assessments that compare students' scores to other students' scores are called norm-referenced assessments. These scores are typically recorded as a percentile. For instance, a student who scores at the 55th percentile scored better than 55% of their peers taking that same assessment and a student who scored at the 99th percentile scored better than 99% of their peers taking that same assessment. Under this method, students frequently move on to the next segment of learning whether they have passed the assessment or not.

When teachers use tests for mastery, however, the variable becomes not *whether* the student passes or fails and by how much, but *when* the student achieves a passing score. When using this model,

> For mastery, the variable becomes not *whether* the student passes or fails but *when* the student achieves a passing score

teachers typically outline a score that is needed to demonstrate the student has "mastered" the material, and if students do not pass the assessment, they receive remediation, then take the assessment again, and so on until they reach the desired score. Students should not move on to the next segment of learning until they have hit the goal for mastery of the current segment.

Strategies for Creating Virtual, Traditional Assessments for Summative Purposes

When we use assessments to compare students to either a predetermined set of criteria or to their peers for the purpose of providing a summative grade, both the validity and the reliability of the test become major issues. We want to make sure the assessment measures *exactly* what it is intended to measure (otherwise, the grade is not meaningful) and that students are following the predetermined conditions under which to take the test. Below are several strategies that teachers can use to control for these factors.

Use Timed Assessments

If a teacher is worried that students are going to look up answers, either on their primary device or a secondary device, consider using an assessment tool that allows control over how long students have to take the assessment. The tricky part is determining *how much* time to give to students; teachers need to hit that sweet spot where there is enough time for students to thoroughly answer the questions while also not giving them time to look up all the answers. Additionally, teachers must accommodate students with special needs to avoid unfairly penalizing anyone.

Create Unique Questions

Think about the questions you can ask Google and get an easy answer. They usually include things like, "Who was the first President of the United States?" and "What is 8×7?" If teachers don't want students to be able to do a quick search on either their primary or a secondary device, then they need to ask unique questions that are not easily entered into a search engine. For example, "Of the following, which president would have been most likely to approve of the current two-party system?" or "If a house has a room that is 8 feet by 6 feet, how much carpeting is necessary to cover the whole floor?"

Require Answer Justifications

One way to ensure that students truly understand the answer is to ask for students to supply reasoning that shows why their answer is correct. Of course, if using a select-response question, this requires the addition of a supply-response item, therefore, introducing a slightly extended grading time and potential subjectivity in evaluating the correctness of answers.

Use Tools That Allow for Item and Answer Randomization

Randomizing question and item order helps to ensure that students cannot easily and quickly message each other to say that "Answer #1 is C." If teachers allow students to retake an assessment to earn a higher score, students cannot simply memorize the location of the answers; at the very least, they have to read the question each time and pay attention to the order of each answer.

Use Tools That Pull Random Questions From Question Banks

Certain testing programs will allow teachers to create "banks" of test items. Teachers can then tell the program to pull "3 questions from learning objective 1" and "5 questions from learning objective 2." This ensures that students cannot quickly share answers with one another, because they may not even be getting the same items. Moreover, if students retake the assessment, they will get completely different items, meaning that they have to truly comprehend the material rather than simply memorizing correct answers.

Use Multiple-Select Items Rather Than Multiple-Choice

A multiple-select question is one in which there are potentially multiple correct answers, and a student must choose all that are correct, unlike multiple-choice, in which there is only one correct answer. Everyone loves multiple-choice because, in the day of hand grading, it was one of the fastest item types to grade. If assessments are being given virtually, however, the computer can grade multiple-select items as quickly as multiple-choice. Multiple-select items are better at ensuring that students truly understand the material, as opposed to simply memorizing it. When combined with randomized item order and answer choices, as well as randomly pulling from a question bank, the probability that students can share answers is very low.

Let's look at how much more difficult a test item can be when it uses unique questions and multiple-select, when compared to a more generic, multiple-choice item.

Traditional Assessment Strategies

Generic/Multiple-Choice	Unique/Multiple-Select

1. Something that is kept the same in each trial of an experiment is called—
   a. A control
   b. A constant
   c. An independent variable
   d. A dependent variable
	1. Johnna is conducting an experiment to see whether paper airplanes fly farther with extra weight on the nose. Which of the following should be kept constant to get the most valid results? Choose all that apply.
	   a. How the paper airplanes are folded
	   b. The distance that each paper airplane flies
	   c. The amount of force with which each paper airplane is thrown
	   d. The type of paper used to make the paper airplane
	   e. The number of paperclips attached to the front of the paper airplane

Have Students Keep Cameras on During the Assessment

When giving a synchronous assessment using an online video platform, teachers may consider having students keep their cameras on. While this does not make cheating impossible, it provides a bit of protection. Keep in mind, however, that some students may have internet connection issues that require them to keep cameras off. For equity reasons, teachers should not take away points for having cameras off.

Add an "Oral Response" Component to the Assessment

Some online video conferencing platforms allow teachers to put students into individual "rooms" while they take an assessment. The teacher can then pop into each "room" and ask the student a live question based on the material being assessed. The teacher can count this as part of the overall grade. Teachers can use answers with objectively correct/incorrect answers, such as "What instrument is used to measure air pressure?" or "Name three events that historians typically cite as causes of the American Civil War." The teacher can also use more open-ended questions with a rubric that helps judge the quality of the answer. For instance, a teacher might ask,

"If you were going to predict tomorrow's weather, what sort of tools would you need and what would you look for to make your determination?" or "Do you think the American Civil War was inevitable? Why or why not?"

Consider Making the Assessment "Open Book"

If you are not testing for factual fluency but rather for deeper understanding, it may be better to make the test "open book," or even allow students to use other resources as well.

> If you are testing for deeper understanding, it may make sense to make the test "open book"

Especially if giving an asynchronous virtual assessment, it may not be possible to ensure that students do not use outside resources, so it may make sense to go ahead and create the assessment in a way that plans for them to use those resources anyway. If teachers choose to make assessments "open book," they should also consider using unique assessment questions that cannot be Googled, and also using a time limit so that students must be familiar enough with the material that they need to keep up with their learning and study beforehand.

Strategies for Creating Virtual, Traditional Assessments for Formative Purposes

Whether an assessment is considered "summative" or "formative" refers less to the format of the assessment and more to how the assessment results are used. In formative assessments, teachers and students use the results to inform future teaching and learning. The teacher may use the results to determine skills that need to be retaught versus those that most students know proficiently. Teachers may also use the results to create student groups. The same assessment can be used both summatively and formatively. For that reason, many of the above strategies for summative assessments may also apply to virtual assessments that are also being used formatively. If the main purpose of the assessment is formative, however, there are several strategies that teachers should consider in addition to those listed above.

Traditional Assessment Strategies

Allow Students to Retake Assessments

If an assessment is being used formatively, the purpose is to inform future teaching and learning, not to give a fixed grade measuring what students know "right now." With a truly formative purpose, assessments

> It does not make sense to take an "average" of the first time a formative assessment is given and the subsequent times

should be used to determine skills that students still lack, the teacher should provide remediation, and then the student should be allowed to demonstrate their newly acquired skills. Moreover, it does not make sense to take an "average" of the first time an assessment is given and the subsequent times. Think about it like this: If a child is learning to ride a bike and falls off the first three times, do parents simply shrug and say, "Well, I guess you can't ride a bike?" Or, if they encourage the child to keep trying and the child eventually masters bike riding, do we say that students can only "Half-ride a bike" because the child fell off in the beginning? Of course not ... because the point is not to grade bike riding, but to give advice each time the child falls, such as "Remember to keep pedaling!" or "Make sure you have your hands on the hand-brakes at all times." That is the heart of formative assessments ... noting what needs to be improved, giving feedback, and then trying again until the skill is mastered.

Now, sometimes we hear from teachers, "But doesn't this encourage students not to learn the material the first time?" At first ... maybe. But once a culture of a true growth mindset is established, most students will want to do well the first time so they can move on to the next skill. After all, no one *enjoys* falling off the bike. This does, however, require a conscious effort from the teacher to build this type of culture within the classroom.

Use Autograding and Immediate Feedback Tools as Much as Possible

If we allow students to retake assessments, then as much as possible, teachers should try to use tools that allow autograding (the tool grades items for you) and provide immediate feedback to the students on not only an overall score, but on individual questions. Some tools not only allow students to see which items they answered correctly ... they also allow teachers to write explanations regarding why some answers are correct and others are not.

Depending on the type of information and skills that students are learning, it may be enough to have students answer the same questions each time. For instance, if students merely need to memorize facts for fluency purposes (such as their multiplication tables), why not let them answer the same questions each time? Although, it is still recommended that item and answer order are randomized to keep students from simply memorizing the pattern of answers. If, however, students are meant to be demonstrating comprehension or application of new learning, it makes sense to use virtual tools that pull randomly from question banks created by the teacher. This ensures that students are not simply memorizing answers.

Grading Virtual Traditional Assessments

Grading virtually presents many of the same challenges and considerations as grading assessments that have been completed in-person. For instance, we still need to be concerned with validity—the extent to which we can infer students' understanding based upon how students perform on the assessment—and reliability—whether testing errors interfere with students' performance. Therefore, when designing a virtual traditional assessment, it's helpful to keep the following in mind.

Develop a Fair Grading Scheme

Frequently virtual learning class sessions do not last as long as in-person sessions, due to the "screen fatigue" that can occur from sitting in front of a screen for extended periods of time (especially if the class is not particularly interactive). Therefore, in order to be able to give synchronous virtual assessments, many teachers choose to give short assessments or quizzes (ten or fewer questions), which is perfectly fine as long as there are enough items to make a valid inference about students' understanding. Unfortunately, however, if the teacher uses these shorter assessments and then grades strictly using percentages, one or two

> In order to be able to give synchronous virtual assessments, many teachers choose to give short assessments or quizzes

missed questions can have an undue negative impact on students' grades. Consider, for instance, the following quiz scores for Student 1.

Student 1

Quiz Number	# of Items	# Student Answered Correctly	Percentage
1	5	3	60
2	10	10	100
3	10	10	100
AVERAGE (MEAN)			86.7%

If, however, we consider that in normal circumstances, this might have been a single 25-item assessment, 23 correct out of 25 questions would be a 92%. Depending on the grading scale for the school or district, simply grading each quiz using percentages, rather than as a single assessment taken in three different sittings, has the potential to drastically lower a student's grades by one or more letters.

Using rubrics requires some of the same considerations, which will be discussed more in later chapters.

Determine What Will Be Considered "Mastery"

Especially when giving formative virtual assessments, teachers may want to determine a score that equates to "mastery." For instance, perhaps being able to answer 18/20 multiplication fact questions in 1 minute can be considered "good enough" factual fluency to move on to the next skill. However, if we give a percentage grade, that would be a 90%, even though the main purpose is formative assessment rather than making a summative determination about student understanding. Nevertheless, some schools or districts require a certain number of grades each quarter. So, how do we reconcile this need for a certain number of grades with the overall purpose of mastery?

One way is to remember that the mathematics behind traditional grading is somewhat arbitrary. There is no hard and fast rule that every assignment must be graded out of 100 percentage points. In fact, some schools do not give number grades at all; they list each skill and give a qualitative rating of how close the student is to mastery (e.g., Beginning, Developing, Mastered, etc.).

Teachers, therefore, have more flexibility in grading than they may realize, especially if everyone on the grade level or department team decides to grade the same way, so that grades are fair across teachers.

Consider, for instance, that a requirement for mastery of fact fluency for a particular unit is set at 80%. Students may take a series of five ten-item quizzes in order to prove mastery, and

> There is no hard and fast rule that every assignment must be graded out of 100 percentage points

they cannot move on to the next quiz until they have answered at least eight out of ten items correctly on the quiz before it. There are a few different ways that a teacher can grade these assessments.

Under the first scenario, the teacher can grade each assessment as either "pass" or "retake." A "passing score" (8/10) is worth 100%, because the student has completed 100% of the requirements for mastery. Therefore, the gradebook would look like this:

Quiz Number	# of Items	# Student Answered Correctly	Percentage
1	10	8	100
2	10	10	100
3	10	10	100
4	10	8	100
5	10	8	100
AVERAGE			100%

If, however, the teachers were to use more traditional scoring methods, the scores would look like this:

Quiz Number	# of Items	# Student Answered Correctly	Percentage
1	10	8	80
2	10	10	80
3	10	10	80
4	10	8	100
5	10	8	100
AVERAGE			88%

Probably some readers at this point are thinking that the first grading scheme, in which 100% was given for meeting the goal of mastery, even if the student only answered eight out of ten items correctly, seems unfair. After all, how is it fair that a student who scores all 100s on every assessment gets the same score as another student who misses two questions on three different assessments? We also sometimes hear teachers say that "that's not how real life works." But actually, there are plenty of instances in which real life works like that. For instance, if the passing score on a driver's test is 80%, the student who scores at 82% gets the same license as the student who scores a 100%. Similarly, in most professions requiring certification, such as medicine and law, there is no appreciable difference in outcomes for the person who scores just above the minimum requirements of mastery and the person who gets a perfect score.

Does that mean that grading for mastery is always the most appropriate grading method? Of course not. The purpose of this section is not to convince teachers to grade only for mastery, but to instead encourage teachers to consider their overall purpose for the assessment they are giving, and then grade in a way that is most appropriate for that purpose. Just as it makes no sense to continue to use a particular method because that's the way "we've always done it," we need to make sure that if we change to a new method, it is because it is the best option for what we are trying to achieve.

Using the Traditional Assessments and Their Results

While teachers generally tend to use traditional assessments for grading purposes, we recommend that any assessment be used for formative purposes as well. To that end, teachers should implement the formative assessment protocol in the following ways when using traditional assessment strategies:

1. **Identify:** First, the teacher must identify the intended learning objectives that are to be assessed. Teachers need to go through and determine which intended learning objectives can best be assessed using traditional assessment methods. Generally, intended learning objectives that assess students' abilities to remember, understand, and apply information work best to

create items for traditional assessments. Traditional assessments can also be used to have students analyze information, but it may be more time-consuming to write items at this level. Intended learning objectives that are written at the Evaluate and Create levels of Bloom's Revised Taxonomy are generally better assessed with a different strategy.

2. **Plan:** When giving virtual traditional assessments, it is very important to plan *how* the assessments will be given. Teachers need to consider whether assessments need to be synchronous (which takes up live class time but lowers the chances that students will not follow the rules for taking the assessment) or asynchronous (which saves live class time but means that students have more access to resources that the teacher may not want them to use). If the assessments are to be given synchronously, then the teacher will most likely want to break them up into smaller chunks, in which case the teacher needs to plan for how the assessments will be graded in a way that is fair for students. Teachers also need to consider whether the assessment will be timed, whether all students will receive the same items or a question bank will be used, whether items and answer choices will be randomized, and whether there will be an oral component to assess student understanding.

> When using traditional assessment strategies:
>
> Identify
> Plan
> Apply
> Assess
> Refine

3. **Apply:** During this stage, the teacher implements the instruction and then the assessment. If this is the first time using the online platform, the teacher will want to make sure that students receive explicit instruction on how to effectively use the platform. This is done so that teachers are truly testing student understanding of the intended learning objectives, rather than testing how well students can navigate a new online platform. If the assessment is being used for mastery or for purely formative assessment purposes, the

teacher may allow the students to retake the student multiple times until the desired score is achieved.

4. **Assess:** If the teacher is using auto-grading software, the actual grading part is far more efficient than grading paper-pencil assessments. That being said, the teacher will want to take advantage of any reports that the software can run. Teachers should consider the following:

   a. What items were most frequently missed?
      i. Were they most likely missed because the item itself is worded awkwardly, does not have a correct answer, or the answer was marked incorrectly in the testing software? If so, the teacher may want to "throw out" these questions and not count them toward students' final grades.
      ii. Were these items missed because instruction on this topic was sparse or missing? If so, the teacher will most likely want to throw out the question(s) for the time being, reteach the material, and then reassess.

   b. What items were most frequently answered correctly?
      i. Double-check to make sure that there was no testing irregularity, such as one item giving away the answer to another item, or an item being constructed in such a way that the answer is obvious.
      ii. If no testing irregularity exists, consider how instruction on this intended learning objective was implemented. What about the teaching methods that can be emulated on other intended learning objectives?

   c. Which students tended to score very high overall?
      i. Do the results tend to generally fit with the rest of their performance on assignments and during classroom discussions? If not, the teacher may want to do some brief oral follow-ups with students. Note: for the sake of fairness, if the teacher decides to do this, they should do an oral component for *all* students, not just the ones whose scores may seem suspicious.
      ii. Consider whether these students perhaps need extra challenges on future units of study.

d. Which students tended to score very low overall?

   i. One thing about virtual assessments that must always be considered is internet connection and potential device malfunctions. Teachers need to give students and families who report technical difficulties extra grace. Otherwise, teachers are grading students based upon their access to high-speed internet and upscale devices, which causes significant equity issues.

   ii. If no internet issues were involved, determine how students will receive remediation. Will they be invited to a small group synchronous class to review missed items? If there are clusters of skills missed, the teacher may want to structure the small group invitations around those skills, meaning that students may be invited to one or more small group sessions.

5. **Refine:** Once the assessment is given, teachers need to look at the assessment as a whole. What worked well? What will need to be changed for next time? If we are sure that the instruction was solid, but the students did not score as well as expected, was there a problem with the assessment platform? If the material is typically very challenging for in-person learners, but students all scored exceptionally well, were there issues with students using disallowed outside resources to find answers? If so, what steps will be taken in the future to ensure that students follow all the rules for taking the assessment? Or, will items that are less likely to be "Google-able" need to be created?

Case Study Example

Identify

Maria Rose teaches a virtual fifth-grade science class. The first unit that she teaches introduces students to the concept of the scientific method. One of her first intended learning objectives requires that students know definitions and can apply concepts for the following terms: experiment, hypothesis, control, constant, independent variable, dependent variable, results, and conclusion.

When teaching an in-person class, she would usually give a 20-item assessment but decides that she will break up the assessment into four separate sessions of five items each that will take place during the last 15 minutes of four different synchronous class sessions. For the purposes of this case study, we will look at the assessment that she gives on independent and dependent variables. One thing that Ms. Rose knows she needs to do is ensure that students understand the definitions of these two words. Therefore, she decides that two of the items on the assessment will deal with the definitions, and the other three items will require students to apply the concepts.

Plan

Ms. Rose decides the first two items will be simple multiple-choice items in which students must match the word with the correct definition. All students will receive these same two items. In order to cut down on the chances that students will somehow share answers with one another, she plans to use a virtual assessment platform that will randomize both the item and answer order.

For the application-level items, Ms. Rose decides to use a question bank. She creates ten items that describe experiments and ask students to identify the independent and/or dependent variables. While she considers making these items multiple-select, she determines that because there is usually only one independent and one dependent variable per experiment (at least for the fifth-grade understanding of experiments), it makes more sense to use multiple-choice where only one answer choice is correct. She sets up the virtual assessment program to pull three items from this set. She is relatively sure that students will not be able to Google these answers, and because students will be receiving different items with randomized answer choices, she determines that the probability of students "cheating" is low, and therefore she should be able to make valid inferences about students' understanding. As one further precaution, she sets a time limit for the quiz for 10 minutes, figuring that 2 minutes per question should be more than sufficient. She has set aside 15 minutes for the assessment so that she can give directions to students beforehand.

Ms. Rose also decides that she will allow all students to take this quiz up to three times because it is crucial that they know this information in order to do well with all successive units. Knowing that she intends to use this quiz for a grade, she sets up the assessment program so that it will allow students to see which questions they got right and wrong, but it will not tell them the correct answers for what they got wrong. This way, students cannot simply memorize the answers should they happen to get the same items on successive versions of the quiz.

Apply

Ms. Rose teaches a lesson on the entire scientific method, having students do an experiment in which they place ice cubes in plastic bags. Each student decides what method they will use to "melt" the ice cube, choosing things like: putting the bag in a window, holding the bag up to a light, hammering the ice cube into shards, putting the ice cube under their arm, etc. While she does discuss other parts of the scientific method (hypothesis, constant, control, etc.), she has students pay special attention to the fact that while they all have the same *dependent* variable (how long the ice takes to melt), they are implementing different *independent variables* (the treatment given to the ice cubes). Each student, in addition to performing the experiment and sharing the results with others, completes a graphic organizer while doing the experiment.

For independent work, Ms. Rose has students watch a series of five "30-second" experiment videos, in which an experiment is shown and described, and students must guess the independent and dependent variables before then being given an explanation about which answers are correct and why. Students then write a reflection explaining their own understanding of independent and dependent variables based upon what they saw in the video.

Because the class meets every other day, Ms. Rose reviews the reflections, provides individual feedback, and then during the next class, reviews some of the most common misconceptions. She has the students play an online collaborative game together to review the terms, and then gives the assessment at the end of the class. Students must keep their cameras on, and she is able to see their answers as they complete the assessment.

Assess

After getting the results, Ms. Rose uses the virtual assessment platform to disaggregate the data. She notes that while 85% of students correctly answered both definition questions, about 30% of students struggled on questions involving the "dependent variables," often confusing them with both independent variables and constants. She invites these students to a small group 30-minute session the following day where she reviews not only dependent and independent variables, but also constants, in order to help students better differentiate between all three concepts. At the end of this class session, these students then retake the quiz. Anyone who still does not score at least an 80% will be invited to stay an extra 10 minutes after the next synchronous class for more remediation, and then will retake this quiz immediately following the next quiz in order to hopefully bring up their grade and demonstrate mastery.

Because this quiz had only five items, Ms. Rose does not give a percentage grade on it. She will instead count it as one-fourth of the overall 20-item "quiz," using the best grade that each individual student received on each quiz.

Refine

When reflecting upon her teaching and assessment for this unit, Ms. Rose decides that while the 30-second experiment videos were helpful, they could have been more interactive if she had used software that not only showed the videos, but stopped at certain points to have students input their answers to identify the independent and dependent variables. She can also mix in some questions about constants into these videos to help students understand the difference. Ms. Rose believes, in addition to a written reflection, this will give her more information regarding which students need more remediation, and what kind of remediation, before giving them the assessment. While she will still do a whole-group review next time she teaches this unit, she decides that she will also add a 10-minute remediation time before class for those students who, according to the video question and answers, need more practice.

Professional Development Plan for This Chapter

1. Bring teachers together, in-person or virtually. They should bring their traditional assessment plan for an upcoming unit.

2. Put teachers into groups of three to four "thought partners" and use the following "Feedback protocol" with these time designations:
   a. For 5 minutes: Thought Partner 1 describes their Identify, Plan, Apply, Assess, Refine elements for the upcoming unit's traditional assessment. These should include the grading scheme.
   b. For 3 minutes: Thought Partners 2–4 ask clarifying questions. These questions should be basic questions that help the thought partners understand the intent of Thought Partner's 1 plan. No feedback should be given at this point. Thought Partner 1 can answer the questions.
   c. For 5 minutes: Thought Partners 2–4 give feedback based on the information in this chapter. Feedback should be in the form of "I like …" in which the thought partner describes what should work well about the plan, and "I wonder …" in which the thought partner makes suggestions or provides additional things for Thought Partner 1 to think about. Thought Partner 1 does not speak during this time, but does take notes.
   d. For 2 minutes: Thought Partner 1 summarizes what they heard and describes their potential next steps based upon the feedback.
3. Complete the protocol for each teacher in the small group.
4. During the groups, the professional development facilitator should visit each group and provide guidance if a group gets off track, as well as acting as the timekeeper.

Virtual Tools for This Strategy at Time of Publication

We know that virtual tools are constantly being created, evolving, and/or being shut down, meaning that some of these tools may have changed since the publication of this book. The following list shows some of the most popular, relatively affordable platforms for teachers, but it is far from an exhaustive list. Moreover, each of these platforms has other features that teachers may find useful that are not listed here. Nevertheless, the following list provides teachers with a starting point.

Traditional Assessment Strategies

Capabilities	Quia	Edulastic	Schoology	Google Forms
Has a variety of item types	Moderate	Extensive	Extensive	Limited
Has auto-grading features	Yes for select-response; minimal for supply-response	Yes for select-response and moderate for supply-response	Yes for select-response; robust rubrics for supply-response	Yes for select-response; allows rubrics but may have to be a separate assignment in Google Classroom
Has a question bank	✔	✔		
Can randomize item order	✔	✔	✔	✔
Can randomize answer order	✔	✔		✔
Shows students their scores	✔	✔	✔	✔
Provides feedback on answers	✔	✔	✔	✔
Has timed tests	✔	✔	✔	
Has reporting features	Moderate	Minimal without subscription	Minimal	Minimal
Has a "grade book" feature to see students' longitudinal scores	✔	✔	✔	Only if used with Google Classroom
Allows students to retake a test	✔	✔	✔	✔
Has a password-protect option	✔		✔	✔
Payment level	Low	Free/Moderate	Free/High	Free

Quick Comparison

Quia is a long-standing website designed for educators who seek to use games and interactive elements as part of their instruction and assessment. While students can access many existing games and assessments for free, teachers who wish to create their own should use a paid account. Accounts allow for activity, quiz, and survey creation based around 16 built-in activity types and 10 built-in question types. These accounts also allow teachers to use their class rosters, create calendars for students, and manage a gradebook. Teachers can also share their activities and assessments with other Quia subscribers, and access the shared materials of the same. Quia does not offer connections to student information systems or learning management systems.

Edulastic provides a strong foundation for teachers using a free account, with important add-ons available for paid individual and district-level accounts. The free version allows teachers to create numerous types of assessments, including technology-enhanced items, either from scratch or from large banks of existing questions. Autograding is available depending on the question type, as are rudimentary reports and hooks to connect assessments to Google Classroom environments. The most notable additions with the paid teacher accounts are read-aloud features, more granular reports, rubric scoring, and a parent interface. The district-level accounts add customizable professional development opportunities, student information system and learning management system integrations, and the ability to work with state assessment data, among other features.

Schoology is a massive learning management system that contains features centered around lesson creation and delivery, student assessment, and data analysis. Teachers and district personnel can build impressive and detailed multimedia self-paced and synchronous lessons and can associate many different kinds of assessments with those lessons, including technology-enhanced items, rubric-based questions, free-response, and more using a free account. The paid district-level plan includes hooks to student information systems, connections to online content sources to which a district might also subscribe, and class rostering and gradebook connections to other platforms. A wealth of on-demand professional development resources is available for all users.

Google Forms is a product initially designed as a quick method of surveying an audience online. However, teachers quickly realized that it could be adapted for simple assessment delivery to students. It features a handful of question types that can be auto-graded and that contain minimalistic formatting and multimedia. Its results are stored in a Google Sheet, and teachers would need to do their own data analysis for anything other than surface-level conclusions. It does not require that students have Google accounts to participate, though a free Google account is required for the teacher to construct and administer the assessments. It can be integrated into Google Classroom for slightly more delivery and reporting options, though it remains simplistic.

Creating, Grading, and Using Classwork and Homework

Imagine how different the world is for young people today. At the same time this chapter is being written, the four-year-old daughter of two of the authors on her iPad. First, the five-year-old has to choose if she wants to play one of her two dozen games or watch a movie or a TV show. Once she decides to watch something, she has to choose from Netflix, Disney Plus, Amazon Prime, and Plex (a program that holds all our purchased movies and TV shows). She chooses Netflix and even on her own account, she has literally hundreds of things to scroll through before making a choice.

The amount of information she has to consider even to turn on *Sesame Street* is astounding, and she has only been on this Earth for five years.

As a survival response to this constant barrage of available information, young people today *are* indeed different from the previous generations. They have had to develop filters to keep this information from being overwhelming, and those filters frequently involve the question, "Is this important for me to do?" and if the answer is "no," then they ask, "Then do I find it interesting?"

Young people then come to school with these filters firmly in place. If a teacher stands in front of them and lectures on the War of 1812 for 45 minutes, expecting students to copy notes as the teacher writes them on the whiteboard, here is what might go through students' brains: *This is not important; I could look up this information anytime I want. This is also not interesting; there's nothing for me to choose or solve or feel emotion about.* (This is not to say that some teachers are not brilliant lecturers; however, a brilliant lecture is even more difficult to give virtually because young people are used to see over-the-top adventures and special effects when looking at screens, and teachers are therefore unintentionally competing with, say, Michael Bay.)

DOI: 10.4324/9781003200093-2

Classwork and Homework Strategies

During the course of our careers, we've seen a lot of outstanding lessons ... and some on the opposite side of the scale. Frequently, the lessons that fail to impress are the ones where students look bored because they are participating in rote memorization, copying information, or otherwise doing work that you can tell they find irrelevant, and we can predict that isn't actually teaching them much. That being said, their teachers usually have the best of intentions. The majority of the time, these teachers thought they had designed the assignments to be helpful to students and easy for students to complete, and are frequently surprised when students don't put forth much effort on said assignments. Then, in teacher training sessions, teachers tell us that students today are unmotivated, disengaged, and have no attention span.

Here is the thing: The world is not changing anytime soon. Because of this, teachers have two basic options: adapt to the way young people learn today ... or continue to use outdated teaching methods that no longer result in more than minimal learning for students. This need for change becomes even more dire when teaching virtually, because students are expected to sit in front of a computer for hours on end, without the usual movement, collaboration, and stimulation that comes from being in a brick and mortar classroom.

> Young people are going to keep those *Important and Interesting* filters in place; they need those filters to survive in today's information-laden world.

This chapter focuses heavily on how to create virtual classwork and homework assignments that will both engage students and help them learn. After students complete these assignments, the question about how to grade them in a relevant way will be explored. Lastly, we will look at how to use the results to create future learning plans.

Creating Classwork and Homework

One thing that we have learned working with teachers and technology is that while there is some overlap between in-person and virtual pedagogies, there are also some very distinct differences. Teachers who ignore these differences during synchronous assignments frequently find themselves talking to a bunch of black screens as students turn off their cameras, and these same teachers hear crickets when they ask a question.

During this section, we will look at three important understandings for teaching and assessing students virtually:

1. Have aligned learning intentions and success criteria.
2. Strive for cognitive engagement with frequent checks for understanding.
3. Consider the Substitution, Augmentation, Modification, and Redefinition (SAMR) model.

The Importance of Aligned Learning Intentions and Success Criteria

When creating an assignment for students, teachers must be intentional about why *this* activity is better than any of the other activities they could have chosen. Otherwise, teachers run the risk of choosing activities that will not accomplish the actual learning goals, leading to "busy work" for both the students who complete the activity and the teacher who grades it. Busy work can lead to a lack of student engagement (Bowen, 2003) and therefore can cause stress to the teacher, wondering why students refuse to put forth effort. It is a vicious, boring, and fruitless cycle. The goal, therefore, is to carefully consider standards in order to determine what kind of assignment best fits: a drill-and-kill for factual fluency or an open-ended question that allows for creative thinking.

For instance, consider the following Common Core Grade 5 Mathematics standard and think about what type of thinking it is asking students to do.

Operations & Algebraic Thinking

CCSS.MATH.CONTENT.4.OA.A.3
Solve multistep word problems posed with whole numbers and having whole-number answers using the four operations, including problems in which remainders must be interpreted. Represent these problems using equations with a letter standing for the unknown quantity. Assess the reasonableness of answers using mental computation and estimation strategies including rounding.

Classwork and Homework Strategies

When we read this standard, we see that it does not require computational fluency from students, but a higher-level problem solving that involves a series of steps. It may help to read the standard more like this:

> Students will:
> a. Solve multistep word problems posed with whole numbers and having whole-number answers using the four operations.
> b. Interpret remainders.
> c. Represent these problems using equations with a letter standing for the unknown quantity.
> d. Assess the reasonableness of answers using mental computation and estimation strategies including rounding.

With the rise in programs that contain question banks full of items that look similar to those on standardized assessments, it is tempting for a teacher to provide students with a series of problems that focus on only one step of the above standard at a time. There are plenty of worksheet generators in which teachers can input the number of and type of problems they want for students, and then require students to circle or click the correct answer. There are also many programs that give students problem after problem in order to practice their skills, and then promise to provide the teacher with analytical information. (We use the word "promise" here not because such programs cannot fulfill their promises, but because the validity of these results can be questioned if students are not putting forth their best efforts due to frustration or boredom.) Below, we see one such problem that could be made by either a worksheet generator or found in a commercial item bank:

> LaRicia plants four rows of corn. Each row has the same number of corn plants in it, and the total number of corn plants is 24.
> Which equation can be used to determine the number of corn plants in each row?
> (Let c = the number of corn plants in each row.)
> 1. $4 + c = 24$
> 2. $4 \times c = 24$
> 3. $24 - c = 4$
> 4. $24 \times 4 = c$

The above problem certainly meets these parts of the standard:

a. Solve multistep word problems posed with whole numbers and having whole-number answers using the four operations.
b. Represent these problems using equations with a letter standing for the unknown quantity.

If teachers are not careful about how they craft their learning intentions and success criteria, they may end up giving students a series of problems like the one above and using that to wholly assess whether students have mastered the required skills. However, the above problem is missing the parts of the standard that involve interpreting remainders, and perhaps more importantly, determining the reasonableness of an answer. The last part of the standard regarding the reasonableness of a solution is crucial, because that portion requires the highest level of thinking for students. Not only do students need to be able to apply computational skills, they need to be able to evaluate the quality of answers given and then communicate their justifications.

One solution, of course, is to require multiple parts to a problem that meet each portion of the standard. For instance, consider the following problem:

> Mr. Thomas teaches social studies to 62 students. He is taking all his students on a field trip using a school bus. Each row on the bus can fit up to four (4) students and there are 15 rows on the school bus. Will he have enough seats on a single bus?
>
> 1. Which equation should Mr. Thomas use to determine how many rows of seats he needs to fit all his students? (Assume that n = number of rows needed)
>
>   a. $62 - 15 = n$
>   b. $15 \div 62 = n$
>   c. $62 \div 4 = n$
>   d. $15 \div 4 = n$
>
> 2. Will Mr. Thomas have the same number of students in each row?
>
>   a. YES
>   b. NO

3. What number of students will remain if Mr. Thomas fills all other rows to capacity?

   a. 0
   b. 1
   c. 2
   d. 3
   e. 4

4. Which number below shows the most reasonable and minimal number of buses that Mr. Thomas will need to safely transport all his students (assuming that no more than four students sit in each row)?

   a. 1
   b. 2
   c. 3
   d. 4

These problems do a much better job at getting most of the standard. They also have the benefit of all being select-response items, so the program can automatically grade all the answers, saving the teacher crucial time. Unfortunately, because they are select response, we cannot know if students actually *understand* the answers, or if they have simply managed to click correctly (perhaps even sharing answers with one another or having a parent or older sibling tell them what to click).

Of course, these *are* the types of problems that students are likely to receive on standardized assessments at the end of their coursework, so they must have exposure to problems like this. Programs that require students to create a series of problems based on a skill can also be useful in that they provide immediate feedback to students, so students do not practice incorrectly and then have to be "untaught" their misconceptions. Some of these programs even tell students *why* their answer is wrong, and direct them back to lessons or videos they can review to increase their understanding. Moreover, they can provide teachers a limited amount of information from which to extrapolate what students know and what concepts require more work. In order to get information on *every* part of the standard, however, it is important in cases like this for a teacher to go beyond select response in order to determine what students are thinking when they solve these kinds of problems.

Take a look at this problem:

> Imagine that you are the principal at our school. You know that the maximum number of students allowed in a fourth-grade classroom is 25. You have 115 students enrolled for fourth grade for the upcoming school year. You currently have three (3) fourth-grade teachers, and need to know if you must hire more *or* move any to other grade levels because there are not enough students to justify having all three teachers. The district does not want to spend any more money on teacher positions than necessary, so that they can use the money to provide other services to students.
>
> Do you have too few teachers, too many teachers, or just the right number of teachers?
>
> Draw a picture that explains how you know this.
>
> Write an equation that shows how you could solve this. Let t = the number of teachers needed.
>
> Write a short letter as if you are the principal, explaining to the district why you do or do not need more teachers. Make sure to explain your mathematical thinking in appropriate mathematical terms.
>
> Assume you now have the appropriate number of teachers for your 115 students. What is the most reasonable number of students to put into each classroom? Why?
>
> Do you have any classes with different numbers of students? Why or why not?

Note: Sometimes when we show teachers tasks like this, they say, "Oh, my students wouldn't be able to do that." And that is probably true ... if they have never been taught how to think creatively, especially with a discipline such as mathematics. In disciplines where students are used to being quizzed on a series of facts that have right and wrong answers, receiving a completely different type of assignment will most likely give them pause. That is why, before teachers give this type of classwork or homework assignment, they will want to make sure that they have appropriately modeled how to tackle such an open-ended problem. It may also be helpful to have students work in pairs before attempting such a problem individually.

Teachers may look at this task and think, "That would take entirely too much time to grade." And it certainly *would* take more time than using auto-grading software. Teachers would, therefore, not want to give 50 problems like the above; that would be tortuous for everyone involved. These kinds of open-ended problems are more about quality than quantity, and a teacher only needs to use a limited number in order to get a full picture of students' understanding on every portion of the standard, including whether students understand what makes an answer "reasonable." Sometimes open-ended prompts must be used in order to truly assess whether students have mastered the standard.

Therefore, we are not saying there is never a time or a place for these kinds of digital worksheets or skill-fluency programs; when used in moderation, and for the right type of standard, they can adequately serve their purpose. However, if overused, they begin to feel like the dreaded "busy work," which can decrease student motivation and actually make the teacher's job *harder* in the long run. For this reason, we tell teachers to study the standards and determine which require factual fluency, which

> Study the standards and determine which require factual fluency and which need creativity or critical thinking—and then create tasks accordingly

need creativity or critical thinking, and which need a bit of all of these—and then create tasks accordingly. This variety between factual fluency and creative- or critical-thinking assignments will help tremendously to keep students engaged in virtual assignments. Understanding the type of thinking that students are being asked to do is critical for crafting learning intentions and success criteria that will effectively assess student learning for each standard.

Crafting Learning Intentions

Motivation increases when we not only know what we are doing, but why we are doing it (Kover & Worrell, 2010). One way to help students understand the why behind their work is to set *learning intentions,* which can, in turn enable students to set their own goals and focus on their own learning (Dishon-Berkovits, 2014). This understanding of their own learning goals can contribute to students enjoying the learning process (Kover & Worrell,

2010), which can help shift student motivation from an extrinsic to an intrinsic process. Engagement can be predicted by the level of student motivation, which also will contribute to student learning and positive academic outcomes (Froiland & Worrell, 2016).

The fact that busy work, especially busy work that appears to have no practical application to the real world, can decrease student motivation and that is why a teacher needs to strongly consider what the standard is truly asking when crafting learning intentions. *Learning intentions* are statements that encapsulate what students are expected to learn from a particular lesson or assignment (Hattie, 2008). According to John Hattie (2008), learning intentions provide students with guidance not only toward *what* they are learning, but also *why* they are learning it. They give students a sense of purpose. Therefore, these learning intentions should be written in language that is developmentally appropriate for students, and, for maximum effectiveness, should be communicated to students multiple times during the lesson.

One important note about learning intentions: The content in the learning intentions is more important than using a particular sentence starter for learning intentions. Districts or schools may require teachers to use language such as "The student will be able to" or "Today I will …" or "I can …." Any of these sentence starters can accomplish the purpose of learning intentions. The power behind learning intentions comes not from how the sentence begins, but from appropriately aligning the learning intention with the standard, explaining what students will be doing, and communicating the learning intentions multiple times throughout the lesson.

> The content in the learning intentions is more important than using a particular sentence starter for learning intentions

Look back at the mathematics standard and the open-ended activity above. Which of the following would be the best learning intention for this activity?

1. Students will be able to:
    a. Solve multistep word problems posed with whole numbers and having whole-number answers using the four operations.
    b. Interpret remainders.

c. Represent these problems using equations with a letter standing for the unknown quantity.
   d. Assess the reasonableness of answers using mental computation and estimation strategies including rounding.
2. I will solve word problems with more than one step.
3. I can solve a real-life style problem by writing the correct equation, drawing a picture that represents the problem, and explaining how I solved the problem.

Of course, each of these learning intentions has its benefits and drawbacks. Learning intention #1 comes directly from the standard itself, and is therefore the most complete of the learning intentions listed. That being said, it does not really explain the activity that is being completed and it is not written fourth-grade student-friendly language. Moreover, it's verbose and therefore difficult for students to remember and take ownership of. If a teacher wants to use this type of learning intention, we recommend that the teacher share each statement separately during the lesson or portion of the unit on that particular skill. The teacher will also need to help students define words so that they have a strong understanding of what those words mean.

The second learning intention ("I will solve word problems with more than one step") is in student-friendly language and is short and easy to remember. However, it does not explain *why* students are doing this particular activity, nor does it explain the majority of the standard. It is easy, but perhaps too vague. It does not provide a strong context for the learning, which is the one of the reasons that we use learning intentions.

The third learning intention could be considered the "Goldilocks" learning intention. It is in student-friendly language and it gives students a stronger overview of what they will be learning and the type of thinking students will be doing. If you read it, and thought it could still be improved: you are most likely correct. There is no such thing as a "perfect" learning intention, and teachers will want to experiment with different styles of learning intentions and ask for student

> There is no such thing as a "perfect" learning intention, and teachers will want to experiment with different styles of learning intentions and ask for student feedback when sharing the learning intentions.

feedback when sharing the learning intentions. If students say they are confused or do not understand the learning intention, either they need more instruction on some of the verbiage (if developmentally appropriate) or the learning intention needs to be wholly reworded. The test of a strong learning intention is whether students can not only repeat it back, but explain it in their own words.

Crafting Success Criteria

If the learning intention can be considered an explanation about "where we are going," then the success criteria explain "How we will know when we're there." As an example, if I say that we are going to a school today, that's the learning intention. When I say that you'll know we're there because you'll see a sign with the name of the school and big yellow buses pulled up along the curb, those are the success criteria. You will know that we have arrived because of those specific indicators. Every adult who has ever driven with a child asking "Are we there yet?" every 2 minutes understands the importance of giving young people these kinds of guide marks; otherwise, young people will be continually wondering whether they've "made it." Younger students may keep asking; older students tend to lose enthusiasm and may find that their spirits are therefore dampened upon arriving at the destination.

Success criteria should explain specific indicators that the students understand the concepts underlying the lesson. Many teachers like to use the phrase, "I'll know I've got it when …" as their sentence starter for success criteria; of course, as with learning intentions, how the sentence begins is less important than the content of the sentence itself. Like learning intentions, success criteria should be very specific and in student-friendly language.

To see the power of success criteria, think about how many people like video games and will play them over and over to beat a level or achieve a higher score. Part of the reason for this is because video games have perfectly clear success criteria: the goal is to avoid all monsters and make it to a particular point in the generated world; or, players need to destroy all the enemies in a given area in a specific amount of time; or, success occurs when players discover who among their group is the "spy." Our brains like specific success criteria because we like crossing objectives off a list, which is why well-written success criteria greatly enhance the learning intentions.

Look back at our standard and learning intention for solving word problems. Which of the following success criteria do you think would be most helpful to students' understanding how they will know when they have been successful?

1. I will know I've got it when I complete the assignment with 80% accuracy.
2. I will know I've got it when I can:
   a. Solve multistep word problems posed with whole numbers and having whole-number answers using the four operations.
   b. Interpret remainders.
   c. Represent these problems using equations with a letter standing for the unknown quantity.
   d. Assess the reasonableness of answers using mental computation and estimation strategies including rounding.
3. I will know I've got it when I:
   a. Solve a problem by correctly figuring out how many buses will be needed on a field trip.
   b. Write a correct equation that uses n to represent the number of buses needed.
   c. Draw a picture that matches the equation and shows my thinking.
   d. Use the appropriate math terms to explain my thinking.

Success criteria statement #1 is something that we often see teachers use, and it tends to be an indicator that teachers are complying with a directive to use success criteria without truly understanding how to use success criteria effectively with students. After all, how well do most fifth graders understand the concept of "80%?" And when the task is open ended, what does 80% accuracy even look like? When the success criteria are vague or do not fit the type of thinking required in the given activity, it does little to help students internalize what they must do to be "successful."

The second success criteria statement, you probably noticed, is once again mainly composed of the standard itself. This shows another common mistake with success criteria: not differentiating them from

> Success criteria should explain not only the tasks that are being done, but give some kind of measure for determining when the task can be considered "a success."

the standards and/or the learning intentions. Success criteria should explain not only the tasks that are being done, but give some kind of measure for determining when the task can be considered "a success." Moreover, standards are written to be understood by educators, not by students, and this particular standard is not written in student-friendly language for a fourth grader.

The third success criteria, while probably also not perfect, gets much closer to what success criteria should look like. It explains the task *and* the measures that will be used to judge students' skills. It also subsumes the concept of "interpreting remainders" into the task of determining how many buses will be needed, so that students do not need to remember as many parts to the success criteria. Note that these measures used to determine understanding do not need to use numbers; they can be qualitative in nature and rely on teacher judgement. In this particular success criteria, the teacher will need to use their expertise to determine whether students have used "accurate math terms." This is why we should always share the learning intention and success criteria with students and then model how not only how to complete the task, but also help students understand any potential subjective measurements of success.

Three Levels of Engagement

Learning intentions and success criteria help educators to create aligned activities and provide students with an overview of what they are doing, why they are doing it, and what success will look like. The next key to effective classwork and homework is to make the assigned tasks cognitively engaging for students. As previously noted, engagement can be even more difficult in the virtual environment, because students are frequently missing the movement, interaction, and other sensory experiences of a brick and mortar classroom. Moreover, bored students can turn off their cameras or be on second devices with relative ease. This makes it all the more important for the teacher to consider student engagement when designing lessons.

> The next key to effective classwork and homework is to make the assigned tasks cognitively engaging for students

Student engagement is central to productive learning (Sanzo, Myran, & Caggiano, 2014). Researchers have lamented the fact that student disengagement is a major area of concern, as Willims (2003) and Cothran and Ennis (2000) found between one quarter to over a half of students are disengaged. This was pre-Covid-19, meaning it is now, more than ever, vital that we understand how to engage students in the learning environment, both through different instructional methods as well as in how we assess our students.

We know that when students are able to communicate what they are learning, the likelihood of those students having stronger learning outcomes is significantly increased (Chappuis, 2005; Marzano, 2006; Stiggins & Chappuis, 2005). Hence, our emphasis on well designed and articulated learning intentions and success criteria, and considering the importance of student engagement in their learning, assessments that are designed in a way that enable students to reflect on their own performance on the assessments are more likely to have an impact on their learning (Sanzo, Myran, & Caggiano, 2014). We cannot overstate the role of students being active agents in their own learning and the power that has on student engagement and success (Sanzo, Myran, & Caggiano, 2014).

One area of particular attention we want to emphasize when it comes to student engagement is the role of relationships in fostering student engagement. Virtual learning is inherently different from in person learning, especially when it comes to developing positive teacher-student relationships. As you will notice throughout our book, we speak to the importance of providing individual opportunities for students to demonstrate mastery, as well as more whole-group methods. While individual opportunities are more time-intensive, there is great value as teacher-student relationships are powerful predictors of student success (Hattie, 2003, 2008). Students who know their teachers care about them are more likely to be more engaged and successful in the class.

Defining Behavioral Engagement, Emotional Engagement, and Cognitive Engagement

Fredericks, Blumenfeld, and Paris (2004) define three levels of engagement: (1) behavioral engagement, in which students are compliant and complete activities but without much thought or interest, and learning is minimal; (2) emotional engagement, in which students enjoy a lesson but again, do not learn much regarding the intended learning objectives; and (3) cognitive engagement, in which students are truly absorbing, connecting, and using the learning in a way that will most likely toward student mastery of the intended learning objectives.

To better understand the three types of engagement using a real-world example, consider the following World Geography standard from Virginia:

Standard WHI.1a:

The student will demonstrate skills for historical thinking, geographical analysis, economic decision making, and responsible citizenship by

a. Synthesizing evidence from artifacts and primary and secondary sources to obtain information about events in world history.

Recommended Experiences:

Prepare a collection of primary and secondary sources related to a unit of study. Examine the sources to do the following:

- Create a graphic organizer that describes how each source depicts a specific point of view about a period of study.

What follows are examples of assignments that could be given on this standard that would most likely result in each of the three levels of engagement.

Behavioral Engagement: A Practical Example

The teacher provides the students with links or files of two primary and two secondary sources on a given topic. Students are expected to have read these sources before the class begins. During the class, the teacher reviews each source using a slide deck, then switches to a spreadsheet. The teacher writes the title of each primary source in the top column cells. As the teacher does this, students are expected to copy everything the teacher types into a sheet of notebook paper with a similar, though hand-drawn table. The teacher then adds "Historical analysis," "Geographical analysis," "Economic analysis," and "Citizenship analysis" as the title in each of the left-most rows. The teacher then reviews the lecture that was just given while filling in each section of the chart; students are still expected to copy anything the teacher writes. At the end of the lesson, students must take a picture of the copied chart to submit to the learning management system, and the teacher uses this for a classwork grade.

We can imagine the results here. A handful of students may enjoy the task. Most students will probably be compliant and dutifully copy, but without much thought to the content. A handful of students will most likely turn off their cameras and walk away. We have even heard of students who record the screen (or use a second device to record the screen if the teacher has disabled screen recording in the synchronous video platform), go back to bed, then watch the video later when they can pause it and take breaks to get snacks, use the restroom, or engage in activities they find more enjoyable.

Some teachers anticipate this, and make the whole lesson into a video that students can watch asynchronously ... still expecting students to copy the notes and submit a picture of their notes. Of course, anyone who has ever done transcription is aware that most people can accurately copy what someone else says without actually paying much attention to the content. However, with a lesson that only requires behavioral engagement from the students, most students neither enjoy the task nor learn much from it.

Emotional Engagement: A Practical Example

In a lesson that has emotional engagement, students have fun completing the task, but do not necessarily learn the intended learning objective from the experience. For instance, instead of copying notes as the teacher had the students do in the example above, a teacher might provide the same resources (the primary and secondary sources, a video or synchronous lecture using a PowerPoint, and an example of notes in the spreadsheet). To make the lesson more enjoyable, however, the teacher allows the students to use an online graphic organizer website to make the graphic organizer visually appealing. Students can even synchronously work with a partner to create the graphic organizer. Students will no doubt find this far more appealing because it is meeting needs for both creativity and interaction with peers. However, students are still not required to put forth much cognitive effort when it comes to the content itself, and once again there is the potential for lower levels of learning.

Cognitive Engagement: A Practical Example

In order to reach cognitive engagement, teachers need to build specific opportunities that require students to process information at a deeper level. This kind of processing generally takes place when students are required to connect new learning to what they already know, or use the information in a new way. Let's look back at our previous example. Once again, the teacher posts the primary and secondary resources in the learning management system and expects students to read them ahead of time. The teacher also posts the lecture, but in 10-minute segments in which students have to answer a question on a form at the end of each segment. After viewing these materials, the teacher tells students to create a 30-second video of themselves explaining, in their own words, the most important historical, geographical, economic, and/or civic points made by the resource. Students also must explain one question they had about the resources. It might be time consuming for the teacher to grade all of these videos, so the teacher tells the students that videos will be "spot-checked" (in other words, the teacher will pick a random video to grade for each student). In this way, students are engaging with the resources on a deeper level than simply reading them. The teacher also requires students to come to class with one question they had about any of the resources.

> Cognitive engagement requires students to process information at a deeper level

During the synchronous class, the teacher explains that students will work together in small groups to create a graphic organizer that includes all the resources and shows how they relate to one another. The teacher allows students to use a graphic organizer design program, but students must be able to justify the graphic organizer that their group chose and why they feel it was the most appropriate visual for the content. Students have 20 minutes to create the graphic organizer as a group. The teacher then randomly changes around the small groups, and students present their graphic organizers to one another in these small groups. Students give each other feedback, and then return to their original groups, discuss the feedback they received, and make any changes to their graphic organizer. Finally, students write a one paragraph description of what ideas were contributed by whom to create their group's graphic organizer. The teacher then grades each graphic group's graphic organizer and each person's individual paragraphs.

As you can see, these kinds of activities make it much harder for students to complete unless they have fully read, understood, and analyzed the materials. The teacher meanwhile has multiple sources of information in order to determine whether and which students truly understand the material. For these reasons, this is an example of an activity that requires cognitive engagement.

Identifying and Measuring the Type of Engagement

One easy way to determine whether students felt behaviorally, emotionally, or cognitively engaged during a lesson is to define each of these terms for students, and then ask them using an anonymous poll. We recommend that the poll be anonymous so students feel comfortable sharing their true opinions. Teachers who choose this method will need to be sure to use the results to make changes to the way they craft their lessons, otherwise students may not give honest opinions because they do not think the answers will make any difference.

There are also less direct ways to ascertain the level of engagement in lessons, and they have to do with what is measured at the end of the lesson. If a teacher only checks for completion without paying much attention to content, it is most likely that the activity stopped at behavioral engagement. If the teacher asks students to rate their enjoyment of a particular activity, or informally measures the number of smiles and positive comments during the lesson, the emphasis for the lesson was most likely on emotional engagement. The only way to truly measure cognitive engagement—whether students have actually learned the intended information and skills—is to provide students with an opportunity to demonstrate this understanding. If the standard, learning intention, and success criteria were all focused on factual fluency, it makes sense for this assessment of student learning to require the demonstration of this factual fluency. If the standard, learning intention, and success criteria instead focus on deeper or creative learning, the teacher must provide an opportunity for students to demonstrate these types of skills in the classwork and/or homework.

You probably noticed during the cognitive engagement practical example that the teacher was collecting small samples of student understanding multiple times throughout the overall activity. While a teacher *can* wait until the end of an entire activity to assess cognitive engagement, we recommend instead that teachers weave these opportunities throughout the lesson and accompanying assignment. This provides several advantages: (1) Students focus because they know they will soon have to show their

> We recommend that teachers weave assessment opportunities throughout the lesson and accompanying assignment

understanding; (2) Frequent checks for understanding break up longer periods of "teacher talk," therefore giving students a chance to use their brains in different ways; and (3) Teachers can use the information from these checks to ensure that students are "on track," and therefore make adjustments as necessary.

Note these checks for understanding can be as simple as asking students to answer a quick question in a chat box, respond to a poll or question, provide a rating, etc ... Moreover, these checks for understanding do not require a grade and teachers can troubleshoot either general trends or simply individual misunderstandings. Checks for understanding should also be short enough that they do not take significant time from the rest of the lesson. Teachers who use frequent checks for understanding often find the engagement level goes up, simply because students are required to interact with the information.

Next, we will discuss how to make sure students are not only interacting appropriately with the content, but also using the available technology in meaningful ways.

Using the Substitution, Augmentation, Modification, and Redefinition (SAMR) Model

Ruben Puentedura began envisioning the SAMR model back in the 1980s (Boll, 2015). He recognized the impact that technology began to have in classrooms (or the potential for that impact), and recognized that in order for that impact to happen, teachers had to teach students to use technology in new and creative ways. Simply substituting a computer worksheet for a paper worksheet does little to prepare students for technology in their personal and professional lives. As technology in our schools evolved, the way that teachers thought about and used technology also changed. Below, we describe the definition and types of activities that would fit within each level of the SAMR framework. It is important to note this framework is more a continuum than composed of discrete categories, and there is some professional judgment involved regarding that category label best fits a given task. Importantly, the goal is not for every technology task to reach the highest level (Redefinition), but to develop each task purposefully and to get tasks of every level into each unit of study (Puentedura, 2020).

Substitution

Puentedura (2020) defines a Substitution task as one in which "tech acts as a direct tool substitute, with no functional change" (Slide 2). Generally, these tasks are nearly as easy to do "in the real world" as they are virtually. As an example, a teacher may post a digital worksheet in a PDF file in their learning management system, and students use a specific program to circle the correct answers on the PDF. Another example is using an online program that gives students question after question in order to review information or skill fluency. (While it could be argued that programs that disaggregate student data for teachers are at a higher level than Substitution *from the teacher's* perspective, unless they have another feature for students, they are most likely at the Substitution level.) One last example is having students copy definitions onto a word processing document. Often these types of activities save no real time and offer no thinking beyond what the more manual task would have offered. These kinds of activities should be used sparingly and purposefully; they also tend to be less engaging for students, and therefore requiring too many of these types of activities for students may lead to decreased student motivation.

Augmentation

Tasks at the Augmentation level have technology that "acts as a direct tool substitute, but with a functional improvement" (Puentedura, 2020, Slide 2). For instance, rather than having students draw a table to record the results of a science experiment on a sheet of paper and then upload photos of their work, the teacher may have students create or fill in the table on a spreadsheet, showing students how they can sort their data more easily this way. Using a spell checker or a grammar checker in a word processing program is similar, because while the task itself is not much different than if the essay were handwritten, there is a functional improvement. Online information and skill fluency programs may be considered to be at the Augmentation level if, instead of simply giving students problem after problem, they suggest resources for reteaching when students choose an incorrect answer. Assigning online rather than paper textbooks can be seen as another example of Augmentation, because such resources may allow students to click links, watch videos, or otherwise interact in a way they could not do with a paper textbook.

These types of activities tend to make tasks easier or more efficient, and most likely offer some features that would not be possible with a more manual task.

Modification

Modification activities use technology in a way that significantly redesigns the task (Puentedura, 2020). Frequently, these types of tasks *may* have been able to be done manually, but it would be very difficult to do them as easily or as well. Consider, for instance, having students make an infographic with clickable links on a given topic. Sure, students could draw an infographic by hand, but with the virtual infographic, now they also have to find, evaluate, and link websites that relate to their topics. They can also work together collaboratively on the infographic at the same time, which is significantly more difficult when drawing by hand. Moreover, students can potentially work together even if they are not physically near one another. These tasks frequently require more creativity and involve collaboration, and therefore have a higher likelihood of cognitively engaging students. Drawbacks to Modification tasks, however, are that they frequently take more class time to complete and more time for the teacher to grade.

Redefinition

In short, tasks at the Redefinition level simply would not have been possible, or even conceivable, without the technology involved. Consider, for instance, having students create a documentary using historical pictures, quotes, and interviews from previous generations who lived through the historical events. There is simply no way to create such a documentary without the use of technology. Podcasts, similarly, redefine the way that audio stories can be told. Another example would be interviewing astronauts who are on the International Space Station, building or programming robots, creating an app, etc … While not all these activities involve creation or collaboration, of course, at least one of those is frequently a major feature. These are the kinds of activities that not only teach students about the content, but also about using technology to achieve their own goals; the skills they get from doing these kinds of activities stay with them and can often translate to college, careers, and real-life. Keep in mind as well that students in

Classwork and Homework Strategies

higher grades are not the only ones who can engage in Redefinition tasks; students as young as preschool can be taught the basics of coding using technology (such as robots) especially designed to be developmentally appropriate for them.

Grading Classwork and Homework

One of the challenges of teaching virtually is that teachers have fewer opportunities to speak to students one-on-one. The technology at the time of publication requires teachers to create an individual breakout room, set up a separate time to meet with students, or rely on written communication, such as email, feedback on assignments, and chat boxes. For these reasons, it may be difficult to ascertain whether students understand the material. Frequent checks for understanding, as described in the Creating Classwork and Homework section, can help teachers keep track of who knows what, but it can still be a challenge. This is why we recommend using the "I Do, We Do, You Do" method before taking a grade on classwork or homework. Simply, during the "I Do," the teacher models the lesson. During the "We Do," students either work together and/or have the teacher's support while working. A grade is not taken until the "You Do" portion, after the student has had the benefit of multiple opportunities to gain the knowledge or practice the skill.

> We recommend using the "I Do, We Do, You Do" method before taking a grade on classwork or homework

To see how this plays out in a classroom, let's consider two different types of standards and discuss how they might be graded. The first is a Common Core English-Language for Grade 3. Then, to get a different perspective, the second standard will come from the Next Generation Science Standards for Grades 9–12 on Matter and Its Interactions.

Grade 3 English Language Arts I Do, We Do, You Do

Let's start by looking at the standard:

CCSS.ELA-LITERACY.RL.3.2
Recount stories, including fables, folktales, and myths from diverse cultures; determine the central message, lesson, or moral and explain how it is conveyed through key details in the text.

In order for students to not only understand the content, but also the type of thinking involved, it is important for there to be consistency between each stage of the I Do, We Do, You Do model. If we do not have this consistency between what we are teaching and how we are grading, we are unfairly grading students' inherent abilities or their background experiences, rather than whether the instruction was successful. Meanwhile, teachers should also consider everything in the Creating Classwork and Homework section as they create learning intentions and success criteria, strive for cognitive engagement, and carefully choose whether the activity will be at the Substitute, Augment, Modify, or Redefine level. The teacher's plan might look something like this:

	I Do	*We Do*	*You Do*
			*can be homework or classwork; teacher will choose based upon student performance on the We Do section
Learning intention	I can: 1. Listen while the teacher reads a fable, folktale, or myth 2. Figure out the moral. 3. Explain why that's the moral	I can: 1. Listen to or read a fable, folktale, or myth using the online library. 2. I can work with a friend to figure out the moral. 3. I can work with a friend to create a slideshow that shows the moral and explains why that's the moral.	I can: 1. Listen to or read a fable, folktale, or myth using the online library. 2. I can figure out the moral. 3. I can create a slideshow that shows the moral and explains why that's the moral.

(Continued)

Classwork and Homework Strategies

(Continued)

	I Do	We Do	You Do
Success criteria	I'll know I've got it when I can help the teacher create a slideshow that shows the moral based on key points from the story.	Our slideshow is complete when: ✓ We type the moral on our first slide, and the teacher confirms that it makes sense. ✓ We choose clipart that represents the moral. ✓ We create two slides that each explain a different part of the text that supports the moral and choose appropriate clipart.	My slideshow is complete when: ✓ I type the moral on our first slide, and the teacher confirms that it makes sense. ✓ I choose clipart that represents the moral. ✓ I create two slides that each explain a different part of the text that supports the moral and choose appropriate clipart.
Measure of cognitive engagement/ check for understanding	The teacher will give students multiple-choice questions (for instance, "Which is the *best* moral for this story?") and have students respond in an informal poll.	The teacher will review each students' slideshows while they work, and visit each group to provide feedback or help as needed. The teacher may also give written feedback on students' slideshows while they work.	Students will work independently, but will have a way to signal the teacher if they need help (whether the activity is being done as homework or classwork).
SAMR level	Substitute/Augment Students will participate in polls and observe how to create a slideshow.	Augment: Students could create similar posters or books with paper, but this makes the task more efficient.	Augment: see We Do

	I Do	*We Do*	*You Do*
Grading plan	Formative assessment only; no grade	Participation grade only; students get a ✔ once they have met all the criteria	A = Turned in work that met the criteria the first time B = Turned in work the first time that required only minor changes to meet the criteria C = Turned in work the first time that required several changes to meet the criteria D = Turned in work that required significant changes to meet the criteria, or work was incomplete *Note: Grading scale will be modified based on Individualized Education Programs (IEPs), 504s, or other special circumstances as necessary*

You'll notice from the above plan that students have two opportunities to see how the activity is completed or to try it with a friend before they are expected to complete the activity on their own, while the teacher formatively assesses them. The teacher expects all students to meet the criteria, and should give the grading scale ahead of time so that students understand the importance of following the success criteria. These success criteria, which of course would be shared with the students multiple times throughout the lesson, function as the checklist that students will use to determine if their slideshow is "complete."

Classwork and Homework Strategies

Students would be encouraged to refer back to the success criteria throughout the lesson in order to determine if they are "on track" or if they need more support. Using success criteria in this way encourages students' metacognitive thinking about their own learning. As students become more aware of their own thinking, they also become better learners (Bransford, Brown, & Cocking, 1999). According to Sanzo, Myran, and Caggiano (2014), self-regulated learners have "an active orientation towards learning" and "when students clearly understand their learning goals, can define what quality work looks like, and self-asses based on the success criteria that has been clearly communicated, student perform at much higher levels" p. 69).

High School Science I Do, We Do, You Do

Students who demonstrate understanding can:

HS-PS1-1. Use the periodic table as a model to predict the relative properties of elements based on the patterns of electrons in the outermost energy level of atoms. (Clarification Statement: Examples of properties that could be predicted from patterns could include reactivity of metals, types of bonds formed, numbers of bonds formed, and reactions with oxygen.) (*Assessment Boundary: Assessment is limited to main group elements. Assessment does not include quantitative understanding of ionization energy beyond relative trends.*)

	I Do	We Do	You Do
Learning intention	Students will: • Watch as the teacher explains how to use Google Draw to create a model of the element He. • Answer a series of teacher-provided questions in which students must make predictions about the element based on its outermost electrons.	Students will: • Work together in groups of two to three students to create an accurate model of a given element in Google Draw.	Students will: • Create an accurate model of a given element in Google Draw. • Create a question that asks other students to make a prediction based on the element, providing both the correct answer and possible distractors.

Classwork and Homework Strategies

	I Do	*We Do*	*You Do*
		• Create two to three questions that ask other students to make a prediction based on the element, providing both the correct answer and possible distractors. • Review at least two other groups' element drawings and answer the group-created questions.	
Success criteria	I can … • Answer all the teachers' questions correctly in the online poll.	I can … • Work in a group to draw an element that has each of the following in the correct position and the correct number: the nucleus, the protons, the neutrons, and the electrons. • Work in a group to create a multiple-choice question that asks others to make a prediction about our element, providing three wrong (but plausible) answers and one correct answer. • Correctly answer the questions about an element from at least two other groups.	I can … • Independently draw an element that has each of the following in the correct position and the correct number: the nucleus, the protons, the neutrons, and the electrons. • Independently create a multiple-choice question that asks others to make a prediction about our element, providing three wrong (but plausible) answers and one correct answer. • Correctly answer the questions about an element from at least two other groups.

(Continued)

Classwork and Homework Strategies

(Continued)

	I Do	*We Do*	*You Do*
Measure of cognitive engagement/ check for understanding	The teacher will ask questions during the "I Do" section and have students respond in the chatbox. The teacher will randomly call on students to explain what to draw for the given element. The teacher will review the results of the informal poll with the series of teacher-provided questions.	The teacher will monitor groups' drawings as they work, providing either oral or written feedback. The teacher will review each of the submitted questions to ensure that they are written accurately, providing feedback and requiring students to make changes when necessary. The teacher will also review students' answers to each other's questions, and use that information to reteach concepts as necessary.	The teacher will review all drawings and provide feedback in either written or oral form. The teacher will review each of the questions to ensure that they are written accurately. The teacher will create an online quiz game using the drawings and questions, and then monitor student participation and answers on the quiz.
SAMR level	Drawing: Substitution Poll: Augment	Drawing: Substitution Poll: Augment	Drawing: Substitution Online "quiz" game: Augment
Grading plan	Formative assessment only; no grade	Classwork grade on both the drawing and the submitted question.	Classwork grade on students' completed drawings and question; Classwork grade on responses to the online "quiz."

Even though the activities are very different, this plan for a high school science lesson contains several of the same elements. Students receive formative feedback multiple times before working independently. The teacher has multiple opportunities to reteach either an individual, a small group, or the whole class. Moreover, the teacher is constantly monitoring for cognitive engagement through the use of the chatbox, verbally calling on students, or using informal polls. Students need to not only pay attention but also produce work that demonstrates their understanding.

A further benefit of this kind of activity is the ownership that it gives students over their own learning: they are creating the questions that are then going to be answered using an online "quiz" game, which will then be used as a classwork grade. The teacher is not expecting students to automatically know how to create strong questions. Instead, the teacher gives students a chance to practice writing questions in a small group, and then reviews students' independent work before creating the quiz grade. Additionally, students can use the learning intentions and success criteria to review exactly what they need to do in order to be successful with both their small group and their independent tasks.

Case Study Example

Identify

Mr. Jiminez teaches middle school physical education in a virtual environment. His sixth-grade class is about to embark on the following standard:

> VA SOL Standard: 6.1 The student will demonstrate and apply mature movement forms in a variety of activities and identify the six components of skill-related fitness.
> ESSENTIAL UNDERSTANDINGS
>
> - Rhythmic movements can take on a variety of different looks, styles, and forms.
> - The ability to dance can be an advantage in a variety of social situations.
> - Creative dance can help develop critical-thinking skills, body awareness, and social interaction.

While Mr. Jiminez knows that he could simply have students watch and then copy some dance moves, he wants his students to feel ownership over the learning in a way that will positively impact themselves and others. Mr. Jiminez believes that physical education should be about helping students create a lifelong love of fitness in a way that makes sense for each individual. Moreover, Mr. Jiminez wants students to complete an activity that goes beyond simply Substitution for an in-person style activity in order to capitalize on the nature of the virtual environment. He also wants to create an activity in which he will be able to consistently monitor whether students are cognitively engaged with their work.

Plan

Mr. Jiminez starts by sharing the unit learning intention with students, "I can work with a partner to create a video with a series of dance movements to an approved song in order to create a class website that features fun dance routines for primary students." Keeping copyright laws in mind, Mr. Jiminez searches the web for sites that feature songs with Creative Commons licenses. He also creates the following checklist of success criteria to help his students complete their videos:

- ❏ Our video is 30–60 seconds long.
- ❏ Our video uses a song that has been approved by the teacher.
- ❏ Our video fits into one of the following categories: standalone dance routine, dance routine with jump rope or hula hoop, dance/yoga routine, or sitting dance routines.
- ❏ Our video features at least four, but no more than ten, independent movements. Movements can be repeated throughout the video.
- ❏ During our video, we narrate how to perform the movements while we perform them on camera.

Apply

Mr. Jiminez begins the unit by showing students some dance routines that meet the above success criteria and having students copy his movements during the routines. Students also engage in whole group discussion to discuss the different types of movements and the benefits of each on overall physical fitness. They also review the following vocabulary words: combinations, pattern, flow, beat, rhythm, and tempo. Mr. Jiminez uses a short online game to make sure that all students understand these terms and can apply them to practical examples.

Mr. Jiminez explains the classwork activity that will take place over a series of three classes. He shares the learning intention and the success criteria with students, and then demonstrates how to make a video using a free online video software program. He directs students to three different sites that have copyright-free music, and requires that students choose music from one of those sites. He puts students into small groups of two to three, and then has them work in breakout groups to plan their videos on Day 1 and film their videos on Day 2. On Day 3, he assigns new small groups and has each group be in charge of creating the following webpages (he has taught students how to manipulate webpages during a previous unit): standalone dance routines, dances with jump ropes or hula hoops, dance + yoga routine, or sitting dance routines.

Assess

Mr. Jiminez formatively assesses his students throughout the entire three-day lesson. On day 1, he watches students as they follow his dance routines, and provides personalized feedback either verbally or through the chatbox. As students work together in their small groups to plan and create their videos, he continually pops into each breakout group to listen and provide help or feedback as necessary. He reminds students of the success criteria checklist throughout the lesson, and watches each dance routine before filming to make sure that all the success criteria are met. Students receive a classwork grade based on their videos.

To ensure true cognitive engagement, Mr. Jiminez also has students write a one-paragraph reflection on their dance routines. The success criteria for this is, "I can explain why our video will keep young students engaged and physically fit by correctly using at least 4 of the following vocabulary words in my reflection: combinations, pattern, flow, beat, rhythm, tempo." He reviews these paragraphs and invites the individual students who still do not seem to understand the words to a 15-minute review class where they play games to review the words and how to use them correctly.

Refine

To refine this task, Mr. Jiminez asks students what they liked about the class assignment and how they think it could be improved. Several of the students say that they wish they could have used more current popular music, and ask, if they do a similar project in the future, whether they attempt to get permission to use parts of the songs. Mr. Jiminez says that can probably be done for future projects, and that he will make sure to give students enough of a heads-up to contact record labels ahead of time. A couple of students say that they really enjoyed creating these videos, and ask whether they can potentially lead some live sessions for younger students. Mr. Jiminez says that he also teaches a Grades 1–2 physical education class, and invites those sixth-grade students who are interested to come and lead their dance routines with the younger students the next week.

Professional Development Plan for This Chapter

This plan can be used for teachers who teach the same content and/or grade level, or in mixed groups (either content and/or grade level). There is value in doing this both with teachers who are familiar with the learning intentions for the lesson, as well as for teachers who are unfamiliar with the topic from an instructional lens. Both provide valuable perspectives into lesson and instruction development.

1. Create small professional learning community groups, approximately three to four teachers. In general, groups larger than this may not allow the time necessary for each teacher to share, as well as for teachers to have substantive dialogues around their lesson plans.

2. Have the teachers within each group share a lesson plan in advance of the meeting, which includes access to the technology tools they will be using in their lesson. Ask the members of the group to review each lesson plan in advance of the meeting, spending

about 10–15 minutes looking at each (including the technology tools) in order to be familiar with the general parts of the lesson.

3. In a meeting with the small group, whether in person or virtual, each teacher should share the learning intentions and success criteria for the lesson, and specifically detail how and in what ways they are leveraging virtual tools in order to support their students' learning. The presenting teacher should also discuss the lesson plan in general.
4. As the team member presents the concepts for the lesson (no more than 10 minutes), the other teachers are tasked with identifying the level of engagement, as well as the SAMR level.
5. Upon completion of the lesson presentation the observing teachers share for 5 minutes their observations engagement and the SAMR level(s) addressed.
6. The presenting teacher will provide a reflective summary of what they heard and how they might use the feedback to strengthen their lesson, specifically to ensure the intended level of engagement is actually being met within the lesson and that their designed activities fit within the intended SAMR level(s).

Virtual Tools for This Strategy at Time of Publication

Capabilities	Google Workspace	Padlet	Flipgrid	Peergrade	Minecraft: Education
Allow students to work independently or in small groups	✔	✔	✔	✔	✔
Allows teachers to provide feedback on student work within the program	✔	✔	✔	✔	✔

(Continued)

(Continued)

Capabilities	Google Workspace	Padlet	Flipgrid	Peergrade	Minecraft: Education
Allow students to export or "publish" their work to be shared with others	✔	✔	✔	✔	✔
Has a built-in grading feature	Google Classroom has limited assignment grading features				
Allow students to provide peer feedback	✔	✔	✔	✔	✔
Payment level	Free/High	Free/Moderate	Free	Low/Moderate/High	Moderate

Quick Comparison

Google Workspace (formerly *G Suite*) is a collection of tools—notably a word processor, spreadsheet, and presentation platform, among others—explicitly designed to encourage collaborative tasks. The simplicity of the tools, paradoxically, is the reason they are ideal for implementing the various levels of the *SAMR* model: Teachers can challenge students in novel ways by requiring higher-level tasks to be completed by exploiting how wide-open the tools are. Such tasks could include the use or construction of multimedia, the use of peer review, and even the use of peer-constructed responses. The ability of each tool to integrate tightly with the others allows for ever-more complex tasks. At their most basic level, the *Google Workspace* tools could be used by a teacher with a free Google account and by students without accounts at all, but numerous benefits accrue with the paid suite, including student email and videoconferencing tools, enhanced security, gradebook integrations, mobile device access, and more.

Padlet is an online collaboration tool that allows users to interact with each other's ideas using text, images, video, and more. This means that teachers can post prompts or other thought-provoking material and task students with responding; moreover, teachers and students can see the responses in real time, allowing for a complex interplay of views. The tool can be used synchronously or asynchronously, making it ideal for both classwork and homework. The free version provides teachers with all they need to get started but limits the number of padlets that can be offered at one time and provides no mechanism to verify the identity of responders. Paid teacher accounts provide a few minor benefits, but the real power is unlocked at the district-level paid service that facilitates integration with learning management and student information systems, has access controls and security features, and allows students to create portfolios of their work. *Padlet* has apps for multiple device types.

Flipgrid is an online collaboration tool that uses video and other multimedia tools to allow students to share and interact. Teachers and students can post short video or audio recordings featuring prompts, discussion points, or other material, and then students view them and respond. As a tool, this allows for peer review and response tasks and student-driven "performance" tasks. Aside from collaboration, teachers could also use *Flipgrid* to create assessment tasks for individual students. Access controls to prevent abuse include whitelisting email domains (if students have district email addresses) and class join codes. *Flipgrid* works on mobile and personal computing devices and includes built-in recording software. *Flipgrid* is completely free for use by educators.

Peergrade unlocks the power of feedback to improve student learning. Using online tools, both teachers and peers can give feedback on prompt responses from students, including those based on rubrics. Teachers control who can give feedback to whom, and about what, and can even give feedback on feedback—helping students to learn how to be constructive and how to focus on interpreting rubrics for their own learning. Rich reports help teachers drop conclusions about gaps in understanding as well as the reliability of rubrics. *Peergrade's* data can be exported to third-party gradebooks and it can integrate with learning management systems. There is no free version; however, teachers can contract for their own classes, or districts can contract for larger groups.

Minecraft for Education is Microsoft's adaptation of the world-building *Minecraft* tool for educational environments. Teachers seeking to rise through the *SAMR* model's levels would find rich, if daunting, territory in leveraging the platform for student work and collaboration. Nearly every facet of the *Minecraft* core experience—constructing objects and environments out of virtual blocks in a shared online world—falls well within the Modification and Redefinition levels of *SAMR*. Challenging students to create what is not possible in the real world, and allowing other students to interact with those creations, can be a complex undertaking—but *Minecraft Education* users have access to a wealth of lesson and assessment ideas and projects for all subject areas from the educator community. The number of platforms for which *Minecraft for Education* is available is increasing, though use of the tool is not free. Districts pay on a per-student basis, and the product is currently tied to the Office365 licensing system.

References

Boll, M. (Host). (2015, April 10). Dr. Ruben Puentedura, creator of SAMR (No. 4). [Audio Podcast episode]. In *21st century radio: Education vanguard*. https://www.21c-learning.com/podcast/education-vanguard-episode-4-dr-ruben-puentedura-creator-of-samr/

Bowen, E. R. (2003). Student engagement and its relation to quality work design: A review of the literature. *Action Research Exchange, 2*(1).

Bransford, J. D., Brown, A. L., & Cocking, R. R. (1999). *How people learn: Brain, mind, experience, and school*. National Academies Press.

Chappuis, J. (2005). Helping students understand assessment. *Educational Leadership, 3*, 39–43.

Cothran, D. J., & Ennis, C. D. (2000). Building bridges to student engagement: Communicating respect and care for students in urban high schools. *Journal of Research & Development in Education, 33*(2), 106–117.

Dishon-Berkovits, M. (2014). A study of motivational influences on academic achievement. *Social Psychology of Education, 17*(2), 327–342.

Fredericks, J. A., Blumenfeld, P. C., & Paris, A. H. (2004). School engagement: Potential of the concept, state of the evidence. *Review of Educational Research, 74*, 59–109.

Froiland, J. M., & Worrell, F. C. (2016). Intrinsic motivation, learning goals, engagement, and achievement in a diverse high school. *Psychology in the Schools, 53*(3), 321–336.

Hattie, J. (2003). Teachers make a difference, What is the research evidence? Retrieved August 31, 2021. http://research.acer.edu.au/research_conference_2003/4/

Hattie, J. (2008). *Visible learning: A synthesis of meta-analyses relating to achievement*. Routledge.

Kover, D. J., & Worrell, F. C. (2010). The influence of instrumentality beliefs on intrinsic motivation: A study of high-achieving adolescents. *Journal of Advanced Academics, 21*(3), 470–498.

Marzano, R. J. (2006). *Classroom assessment & grading that work*. ASCD.

Puentedura, R. (2020, January). *SAMR: A Research Perspective*. Ruben R. Puentedura's Blog. http://hippasus.com/rrpweblog/archives/2020/01/SAMR_AResearchPerspective.pdf

Sanzo, K. L., Myran, S., & Caggiano, J. (2014). *Formative assessment leadership: Identify, plan, apply, assess, refine*. Routledge.

Stiggins, R., & Chappuis, J. (2005). Using student-involved classroom assessment to close achievement gaps. *Theory Into Practice, 44*(1), 11–18.

Willims, J. D. (2003). *Student engagement at school: A sense of belonging and participation*. OECD.

Virtual Discussion Strategies

Frequently, virtual teachers use discussions to help students collaborate and feel a part of a community. Typically in online learning, students are not in the same location, but nevertheless have the same needs for belonging and interaction. As we discussed in Chapter 2, relationships are a critical factor in students' learning success (Hattie & Yates, 2013). Perhaps, given the "distance" that is a part of virtual learning, it is even more critical for teachers to establish positive relationships and promote a sense of belonging with their students. Students who do not feel they belong in their class or school may tend to be more absent or be disruptive (Finn, 1989). Further, students who feel connected to their school have been found to have more academic success, as well as to have positive behavioral and psychological outcomes (Anderman, 2002). Not only do individual students do better academically and social-emotionally if they feel they belong to their class and school, schools themselves have more positive outcomes as a whole (Anderman, 2002; Johnson, 2009; Osterman, 2000).

Discussions can take place live or asynchronously, and they may be done verbally or in writing. Discussions can be excellent ways for teachers to determine not just whether students remember and understand the material, but whether the students can apply, analyze, and evaluate the content. Moreover, when done well, discussion boards can be highly motivating for students. Consider, for instance, that most social media sites are actually giant, more free-form discussion boards. We know that social media is a pervasive component of many of our students' lives and most are already familiar with dialog back and forth in the online sites. Engagement on these sites release dopamines, which are neurotransmitters, and linked to types of behavior associated with reward actions (Burhan & Moradzadeh, 2020). We can leverage their experiences around social media and craft engaging discussions to help our students learn course content. Rather than fighting against the overwhelming inclination for many of our students to be on social media, we can harness their familiarity with it to encourage learning.

Teaching students how to have thoughtful, reflective online conversations is crucial today. Unfortunately, it is not a skill that is frequently taught. One of the benefits of virtual teaching, therefore, is that it provides a ripe opportunity for teachers to overtly teach these very important skills. This chapter will first discuss how to create both written discussion boards and verbal discussion experiences that give students the chance to use higher-order thinking skills ... while also teaching them how to interact and disagree constructively with others. After that, this chapter will look at how to grade these different types of discussions. Lastly, a case study will show what this process looks like from start to finish.

> How to have thoughtful, reflective online conversations is crucial today. Unfortunately, it is not a skill that is frequently taught

Creating Online Discussions

While scrolling through social media, one of our authors found the following quote from a grad student friend explaining her usual discussion board answer strategy, "Sonia, you make an excellent point. Here is how I am going to restate it so I don't have to do more work, but still receive full credit." Sure enough, this is how most students will approach discussions unless the teacher takes steps to ensure that does not happen. This next section will explain ways to create written and verbal discussions that are more than *pro forma* busy work for students.

Creating Written Discussion Boards

While some written discussion boards may take place in real-time [think of an Ask Me Anything (AMA) session on Reddit], the majority will take

Virtual Discussion Strategies

place asynchronously. Discussion boards are frequently used to ensure that students have completed other asynchronous tasks, such as watching videos or completing their reading, in a way that does not take up precious synchronous class time. Students frequently realize this is the purpose of discussion boards, and may do the bare minimum engagement required to achieve the grade they want. There are, however, several things that teachers can do in order to make the discussion board not only a review of material, but also an engaging learning tool.

> There are several things teachers can do to make the discussion board an engaging learning tool

Ask Open-Ended Questions That Require Application of Knowledge in Interesting Ways

If all discussion board questions require a summary of the content explored, then they do not really fulfill the point of a discussion board; students could more easily submit a one-page reflection or similar. The purpose of a discussion board is to have students exhibit cognitive engagement, which means there must be something that invites a bit of controversy. In other words, the best discussion questions require students to analyze or evaluate something using the facts that they have learned.

Consider, for instance, the following examples of more open-ended questions that still require students to justify their stances:

Grade/Content	Less Interesting	More Interesting
Grade 4 Mathematics	Jordan is going to buy her mother a scarf and gloves. Jordan has $20.00. She wants to buy a scarf that is $14.99 and gloves that are $7.99. Does she have enough money? How do you know?	Write a word problem using addition and/or subtraction, and then provide a WRONG, yet plausible, answer. Your classmates will try to figure out not only the correct answer, but what was done to get the incorrect answer.

Grade/Content	Less Interesting	More Interesting
Middle School Science	What do you think is the most interesting thing about Mars? Why?	Do humans have "right" to travel to Mars? Is it a "duty" that we travel? Why or why not? Justify your answer with at least three scientifically relevant facts about the solar system that you learned during this unit.
High School English	Why do you think that Hamlet believed that his uncle killed his father? Provide three examples from the text.	Did Hamlet see a real ghost ... or was it a hallucination that "confirmed" what Hamlet already wanted to believe? Justify your position with three pieces of evidence from the text.

Providing these types of questions provides motivation for students to answer questions because they help to release some of the same neurotransmitters as social media posts. As mentioned earlier, social media releases dopamines, which triggers a sense of satisfaction and reward (Burhan & Moradzadeh, 2020). The addictive nature of these types of neurotransmitter releases makes it difficult for students—and people in general—to limit social media (D'Arienzo, Boursier, & Griffiths, 2019).

Provide Very Clear Success Criteria

We discussed success criteria in the previous chapter, and this concept is equally important when creating discussion boards. In order for students to know what counts as "acceptable" for both their original post and any potential responses, the instructor should spell out the requirements. For instance, is it enough for students to write a single sentence? Can they use bullets? Or are they providing one or more paragraphs to show their thinking? Do they need to cite their sources, or are they only providing their opinions?

In our experience, when teachers do not provide these kinds of success criteria, students tend to do the least amount of work possible. Of course, in a perfect world, the questions would be so motivating that just like on a social media forum, people would continually check for updates to their own posts without any sort of grade incentive. Here are some examples of success criteria for discussion boards:

- Primary Grades: Write one complete sentence that explains your answer. Make sure to start your sentence with a capital letter and end it with a period. (Sidenote: Teachers will want to make sure to read this aloud to students or provide an option for the discussion board program to read it aloud to students).
- Upper Elementary/Middle Grades: In your three to five sentence paragraph, make sure that you include at least three (3) relevant facts from this week's readings and videos. Reply to two classmates' responses with at least one sentence and explain: (1) whether you agree with them; and (2) why or why not.
    - Missing sentences = 10 points per sentence
    - Missing facts = 10 points per fact
    - Missing/incomplete replies to classmates = 10 points per reply
- High School: Respond to the prompt in a five to eight sentences response. Make sure to cite any evidence from the sources provided as a part of this week's readings; you should include at least three (3) pieces of evidence. You should also include at least one outside resource that meets the expectations for quality sources. Lastly, make sure that you reply to at least two classmates' responses with a three to five sentences response that explains whether you agree with them and why/why not.
    - Missing sentences = 10 points per sentence
    - Missing/incorrect/incorrectly cited evidence = 10 points per piece of evidence
    - Missing/incomplete replies to classmates = 10 points per reply

Additionally, it is helpful to model what an appropriate response looks like. Put the response next to the success criteria, and have students point out which parts of the response meet the various criteria.

Virtual Discussion Strategies

A quick note: Some teachers may prefer success criteria that feature positive language, rather than what points are deducted for missing elements. (For instance, each sentence = 15 points; each correct and relevant fact = 10 points, etc.) While this is a perfectly acceptable method, it has been our experience that it actually takes more time to grade in that fashion because teachers are looking for and adding all the elements that are present, rather than simply counting the ones that are not. Teachers should find the system that works best for them and use it consistently with students.

Require Two Different Due Dates

In every class, teachers will almost inevitably have some students who like to get all their work done early, and others who complete everything at the last minute. If teachers only require one due date for their discussion board (say, Sunday at 6pm), then frequently all the replies to classmates' responses will end up on the first handful of responses. Meanwhile, those who do

> Students who get all their work done early frequently get all the replies

their responses at the last minute will garner no responses. Therefore, the same people continually get replies to their responses, whereas the last person to turn something in never receives replies.

Fixing this problem is quite simple: It requires one due date for students' original responses, and then another due date for them to reply to classmates. For instance, if students must post original responses by Sunday at 6pm, then make their replies to classmates due by Monday at 6pm. This allows the early birds to go back and reply to those who tend to do their work at the last minute, and is more likely to ensure that all responses receive replies.

Require Students to Post an Original Response Before Viewing Others' Responses

Depending on the discussion board platform they are using, teachers may or may not be able to do this particular strategy. Nevertheless, it is one that students frequently find helpful and can encourage more thorough responses *and* the likelihood that students do not simply reword others' answers. If students can see each other's responses beforehand, there are typically two types of reactions students have: (1) some students will happily paraphrase what others have said, rather than actually crafting an original response, and; (2) other students, fearing the teacher may think they are only paraphrasing, will rack their brains trying to come up with responses that are significantly different from what others have posted, sometimes to the detriment of response quality.

For these reasons, teachers should enable any setting that withholds classmates' responses until the student submits their own original response. If no such setting exists on the platform the teacher is using, teachers should suggest to students they prepare their answers by a certain date on a word processing program (such as Google docs or Word), check these responses simply for completion rather than quality, and then have everyone post their responses to the discussion board within a 24 hour period. Students can then proceed to reply to classmates after the 24 hour period has passed.

Teach and Require the THINK Strategy

Anyone who has seen how the majority of people respond to each other on social media knows there can be a lack of decorum in online discussions, especially when two people have differing views. For this reason, it is incumbent upon teachers today not only to ensure that students have the required content knowledge, but also that they have strong written communication skills when interacting with others online.

One strategy we frequently use with students is the THINK Strategy. THINK is an acronym encourages students to consider the following before posting:

1. Is your response **T**rue? (Do you have evidence from reputable sources; i.e., not just a cool meme or sources typically regarded as biased one way or another?)

2. Is your response **H**elpful? (Does it provide a new perspective or facts on the original post?)

3. Is your response **I**nspiring? (Is it worded in a way that will actually cause others to think about the new perspective that you have

introduced ... or will your wording immediately turn off those with a different point of view?)
4. Is your response **N**ecessary? (Will it actually help anyone or provide a new perspective on the topic ... or are you posting it simply to amuse yourself [also known sometimes as trolling]?)
5. Is your response **K**ind? (Does your response convey the same sort of respect that you would like from others?)

In addition to sharing this strategy with students, it is often necessary to demonstrate to them *how* to respond to others who have a different perspective. People frequently see different points of view as a personal affront; on the contrary, they are reminders that no one has all the answers and that we are all of us smarter than any one of us. People with different beliefs generally come by them honestly, and rather than dismissing alternative viewpoints as less informed than our own, we should seek to understand *why* the person has come to a different conclusion. This sort of openness is not most people's natural instinct, however, and therefore teachers must explicitly teach these kinds of skills.

> It is often necessary to demonstrate to students how to respond to others who have a different perspective

Creating Verbal Discussion Opportunities

Too often we have seen teachers put students into an online breakout room with the task to discuss the current topic, only to have students stare blankly at one another. One student may half-heartedly attempt the conversation, while other students may simply turn off cameras and walk away for the duration of the conversation. Similarly, even in whole group discussions, it is not uncommon for the teacher to ask a question and hear crickets in response. Never fear, however, as there are several strategies that can be implemented to ensure that any verbal discussions result in vibrant, thoughtful conversations that help deepen students' understanding.

Virtual Discussion Strategies

Make It Interesting

As we have discussed in Chapter 2, young people today are adept at filtering out any information or task they don't immediately see as "interesting" or "important." While the teacher may obviously think that anything they assign should be considered "important," many of our young people are savvy enough to realize that in the greater scheme of things, a teacher is unlikely to fail them for not wholly participating in a discussion…especially if the discussion is clearly a time filler for the class.

One of the best ways to combat the half-hearted student discussion, therefore, is to use an intriguing discussion starter. We like to imagine: Is this something we would like to debate over the dinner table? If not, then students are unlikely to want to discuss it, either. For instance, which of the following questions would *you* rather discuss?

> Is this something that we would like to debate over the dinner table?

1. Why did the framers of the U.S. Constitution add the First Amendment? OR
2. What should be the limits of free speech? Should people be allowed to say anything they want at any time to any person? Why or why not?

Now, history teachers may think the first question is just as interesting and important as the second question, and surely, it is essential that students understand history in order to interpret the present. While professional historians could no doubt have a field day with question one, the answer set for this question at the K-12 level is relatively limited. There are a few correct answers that students will name and then the discussion will most likely dry up.

The second question, however, will intrigue students because it will require not only their understanding of content, but also their own opinions and experiences. Older students may also be able to add information they know from court cases and/or historical events. There is no right or wrong answer, which is why we still see this question debated in politics today. It is an infinitely interesting question because it examines what happens when generally accepted morals (personal freedom versus the collective good) come into conflict with one another.

In other words, if a teacher wants a robust discussion, the first step is ensuring the question is meaningful to the students on a personal level.

Have a Purpose Beyond Just "Discussion"

If the question itself is particularly intriguing, it may be enough to give the question and let students debate the answer. In cases where the teacher cannot come up with such a question, however, it helps if the discussion has a purpose beyond simply talking. If students are discussing in small groups, teachers can let students know beforehand that someone (or multiple people) from their group will need to share out their responses. While better than not having any outcome for the discussion, this particular task still may not inspire students to "put their all" into the discussion; students may just do enough to have an acceptable share out response before turning off cameras and going to get a snack.

One way to combat students contributing the "minimal acceptable effort" to discussions is to give students an authentic task that requires discussion, rather than just giving them a question. It goes without saying, of course, that the task should be interesting. For instance, consider the following two questions/tasks:

1. What are some ways that we use perimeter? What are some ways that we use area? OR
2. Design the outline of a perfect room for two siblings to share with the minimal amount of conflict using a shared Google Drawing (i.e., a bird's eye view of the shape of the room itself). It must be one room that is a polygon (though it need not be a regular polygon), and cannot have a perimeter of more than 60 feet or an area of more than 200 square feet. Be ready to explain your thought process in creating the room. Students will then vote on which room *they* would most like to live in. Rooms that do not meet the above criteria will not be eligible for the vote.

The problem with Question 1, even if students know they are expected to "share out" after a small group discussion, is there's no real reason for students to listen to one another. Even if they keep their cameras on and not simply trained on the ceiling fan, teachers can frequently tell that students are not particularly engaged in listening to their classmates if there's no real reason to do so. Using a task like #2 above ensures that students not only complete their own work, but also listen critically to the presentations from the other groups as well.

Model and Use Sentence Starters

Once a teacher has crafted an interesting discussion prompt that also requires students to complete a task beyond the discussion, the next step is to make sure students know how to actually participate in a discussion. Young people today may be used to communicating on social media and having discussions about football games or movies, but attempting to verbally wrestle with new content on a deeper level may challenge some of their conversational skills. This may be especially true if they are used to classes where their main function is to be receptacles into which the teacher pours information, rather than being expected to think critically and creatively.

To that end, we recommend that teachers model their expectations for verbal conversations ahead of time. This modeling can take many forms. For instance, the teacher may ask a particularly engaged student to role-play a conversation on the current content. Playing a video in which two people have a rational discussion can also help, especially if the teacher then asks students to explain what each participant in the video did to help the conversation. No matter how the teacher models the appropriate skills, it is important to point out what each person does to keep the conversation moving forward in a productive manner.

> The next step is to make sure that students know how to participate in a discussion

On the other hand, the teacher can also provide students with examples of what *not to do* during a discussion. If role-playing a discussion with a student to demonstrate poor conversational skills, we recommend that the teacher be the one to make the mistakes. This helps ensure that the teacher can intentionally demonstrate "conversation-killer" or "argument-ignitor" phrases. After each modeled discussion, the teacher should have students debrief "what went wrong" and then model how the conversation *should* have gone.

During the modeling phase, it is also helpful if the teacher provides students with conversation starters and continuer phrases. Figures 3.1 and 3.2 below show what some of these may look like. Using these phrases during modeling and then giving students a "cheat sheet" of these phrases during their own conversations can help students who are not used to having robust discussions about content.

Figure 3.1 Conversation starters

In addition to modeling how to use conversation starter phrases, the teacher may have students write down a list of their own conversation starts before the actual discussion. This can help students not only begin a conversation, but slightly change topics once the first question has been discussed in-depth.
- Why do you think that …
- What do you think would (have) happen(ed) if …
- I tend to (dis)agree that _____, but wonder what you think.
- What do you think was most important …
- If you had to rank X, Y, and Z in order of _____, how would you rank them?
- Is _____ always true? If not, what are some situations where it isn't?
- What does X mean to you?
- How has X impacted your own life?

Figure 3.2 Conversation continuers

Just like with the conversation starters, the teacher will want to model how and when to use the various conversation continuers.
- Can you tell me more about why you think/feel that?
- I have a slightly different opinion…
- That's a great point. In addition, I think that…
- I wonder what you think about _____.
- Would you feel the same in X context?
- Would your opinion be the same if…?

As students become more adept at having these types of rich discussions, they can even help to create other conversation starters and continuers.

Eventually, of course, with enough practice, they will no longer need a cheat sheet of phrases.

The last important thing a teacher should demonstrate to students is how to respectfully end a conversation by thanking the other people/people for their contributions. Understanding how to put aside and move on from any differences of opinion that came out during the conversation is an important step in having mature debates. Hopefully, with enough modeling, the next generation will be able to have positive and informative conversations, even when they do not necessarily agree with one another.

Have Patience

One of the things we often hear from teachers is how young people today do not want to interact on screen. Understandably, teachers find this frustrating, especially when they have put much time and effort into creating lesson plans that allow for student interaction. On the other hand, we have seen many students similarly complain that they are rarely or never required to interact, so they learn to "tune out" in an attempt to save themselves from boredom. These students report that as long as they aren't distracting to others, their teachers don't seem to notice whether they are even listening. Older students who have received lecture-heavy lessons for several years will be even more inclined to automatically engage in classes as minimally as possible, because that's what they have been trained to do.

Therefore, we urge teachers not to think of any student reticence for discussion as a fault of the young people, but rather as a skill they have not yet been taught … or that their abilities to immediately tune out are habits that need to be "untaught." New skills take time to master, just like habits take time to break. If a teacher cautiously tries to start one conversation and it falls flat, that doesn't mean that the teacher should give up … it simply means that more explicit instruction on the art of conversation is required.

This is why we tell teachers to have patience. Scaffold the learning. Don't expect the students to have Socrates-level discussions the first day, week, or even month out. Start small, with short conversations. Provide feedback to students on not only to their understanding of the content, but also to their conversational tactics. Continue modeling as long as is appropriate. With enough time, effort, and interesting discussion prompts, students will eventually become excited to come to your class, because they know that they will get to have rich interactions and discussions on important topics.

Grading Online Discussions

It may seem strange at first to grade discussions, and we do not recommend simply assigning students a letter grade. Especially in a world in which the majority of students' conversations may take place on social media, teaching students the art of conversation requires letting them know what they are doing well and where they need to improve. For those of us who grew up in a time before everyone had a personal device (or more than one, in many cases these days), the idea that young people need deliberate instruction and feedback on how to hold a robust conversation may feel ridiculous, or not part of your job as a teacher. The fact remains, though, that if students have gotten to your classroom without this ability, then they are likely not learning the art of discussion outside of school. So where and when *will* they learn it, if not from you? As teachers, it is our responsibility not merely to teach content, but to help students be successful beyond PreK-12 education. Being able to articulate ideas, ask clarifying questions, and disagree productively are all essential skills for any workplace or relationship. To that end, in addition to giving students clear success criteria before they begin the discussion, we also recommend using a checklist or rubric to provide feedback. In the next few sections, we explain how to use each to provide feedback, and possibly even a grade, on student discussions.

> Being able to articulate ideas, ask clarifying questions, and disagree productively are all essential skills

Differences Between Checklists and Rubrics

While educators sometimes use these terms interchangeably, checklists and rubrics serve different functions[1]. Checklists work best when grading objective criteria, whereas a rubric should be used any time that professional judgment is required. Grading a checklist goes quickly, but rubrics require more time on the part of the teacher *because* professional judgment is required. Checklists use objective criteria and therefore rarely require additional specific feedback from the teacher. To use a rubric well, on the other hand, the teacher should provide evidence regarding the given grade. Rubrics take longer to grade, which is why we recommend *only* using them when professional judgment on the quality of work is required. For both rubrics and checklists, however, we strongly recommend sharing the checklist or rubric with students beforehand, as well as giving them practice using the checklist or rubric themselves. Demonstrating model answers and allowing students to engage in practice discussions can help students better understand how to use the checklist or rubric. When implemented successfully, both a checklist and a rubric can provide valuable feedback to the learner.

Using Checklists

Teachers and students alike tend to enjoy checklists because they make grading easy. Checklists provide clear, specific criteria. When the teacher provides the checklist to students ahead of time, students know exactly what they must do in order to be successful. Checklists can be used for either written or verbal discussions, depending on the goal of the particular discussion. The simpler the goal, the more appropriate the use of a checklist.

Checklists and Written Discussions

Teachers frequently use written discussions online to ensure that students have completed assigned reading or viewing of materials. A discussion board with strong prompts is a quick way to do this while also giving students a chance to interact and make connections to the material. For instance, consider this example of a discussion board for Grade 4 science students:

Prompt

Do you think that Galileo was right to recant his statements that the Earth revolves around the sun? Include at least three facts from this week's assigned reading to justify your answer. Reply to at least three classmates' responses explaining why you agree or disagree with them.

Success Criteria

❑ Answer is written in complete sentences in a paragraph that is five to eight sentences long. (20 points)
❑ Answer contains at least three facts from the reading. (20 points each × 3 = 60 points)
❑ Responds in complete sentences to at least two classmates explaining reasons for agreeing/disagreeing. (10 points each × 2 = 20 points)

Using a checklist like the one above, and indeed including it right in the prompt itself, helps students know exactly what they must do to be successful. It also allows students to figure out their own grade, and to easily understand any grade they receive on the assignment. It is also faster to grade than a rubric.

Nevertheless, we often see teachers put criteria like this into a rubric, which frequently takes up more space and more cognitive energy for both the teacher and student to process. Such a rubric frequently looks something like this.

Category	Unacceptable	Needs Improvement	Proficient	Excellent
Sentences	Does not use complete sentences (0 points)	Contains one to two complete sentences (10 points)	Contains three to four complete sentences (15 points)	Contains five to eight complete sentences (20 points)
Ideas	Uses no ideas from the reading (0 points)	Uses one idea from the reading (20 points)	Uses two ideas from the reading (40 points)	Uses three ideas from the reading (60 points)

(*Continued*)

(Continued)

Category	Unacceptable	Needs Improvement	Proficient	Excellent
Responses	Does not respond to classmates (0 points)	Replies to one or more classmates but responses are not three to five sentences in length (5 points)	Replies to one classmate in a three to five sentences response (10 points)	Replies to two classmates in a three to five sentences response (20 points)

While this rubric and the checklist measure the same things in almost exactly the same ways, the rubric has far more words, therefore, making it more cumbersome for both the student and teacher to use. For this reason, when criteria are either present or not (such as whether the student does or does not use ideas from the reading), we recommend using a checklist because it is easier for students to process and quicker for the teacher to grade. Grading discussions can be time consuming, and for that reason, we always advocate for efficiency wherever possible and appropriate.

Checklists and Verbal Discussions

Checklists can also be used for verbal discussions. Grading verbal online discussions can prove challenging if the teacher uses multiple small groups in concurrent breakout rooms, and a checklist may make it easier for the teacher to pop into one group and listen to a discussion for, say, 5 minutes before moving on to another group. Again, letting students know the success criteria on the checklist beforehand and showing them examples and nonexamples of meeting the standards, can help students when they then engage in the discussion themselves. Teachers may also find it helpful to allow students some "practice discussions," in which the teacher tells students what grade they *would* have received, and provides feedback for the next discussion. This may especially help students who are shy or not confident in their discussion skills.

Teachers will need to determine ahead of time what specific criteria they are looking for. Because these are checklists, the criteria should be more objective (i.e., things that are either present or absent). We also recommend using checklists before implementing rubrics. Checklists can help students learn the elements that should be present in their discussions, and then rubrics can help students work on the quality of those elements.

A checklist for a primary online classroom may look something like the table below, while a checklist for a classroom of older students may look something like the following one. Note that we suggest that when working with younger students, they should practice their discussions in pairs before moving on to bigger groups, where the dynamics are necessarily more complex. This is also recommended for older students who have not participated in online discussions frequently.

Primary Classroom Discussion Checklist

Did I ...

❏ Look at the screen when both my partner and I talked?
❏ Talk loud enough for my partner(s) to hear?
❏ Listen carefully to my partner(s) when they spoke?
❏ Speak when it was my turn?
❏ Only talk about the topic my teacher gave me?
❏ Make sure that my partner had a chance to speak?

Upper Elementary and Secondary Classroom Discussion Checklist

---

Did I ...

❏ Keep my attention on the discussion the whole time? *(0–10 points)*
❏ Speak clearly? *(0–10 points)*
❏ Keep my camera on and focused on me? *(0–10 points)*
❏ Stay on topic? *(0–10 points)*
❏ Use open and encouraging body language? *(0–10 points)*
❏ Ensure that any conflict of opinion was productive? *(0–10 points)*
❏ Ask clarifying and/or probing questions as appropriate? *(0–20 points)*
❏ Ensure an equitable expression of viewpoints between myself and my partner(s)? (i.e., I neither spoke too much nor too little) *(0–20 points)*

Readers will notice the primary rubric has no scoring guide, whereas the rubric for upper elementary and secondary students does. This is because we recommend teachers provide feedback rather than grades to primary students. We also recommend teachers do not issue grades for upper elementary and secondary students until students have had multiple opportunities to practice these skills and receive feedback with the checklist ... if teachers give grades for discussions at all. Teachers may also choose to emphasize different skills with their grading schemes for this checklist.

Lastly, and somewhat contradictory to our previous advice, we encourage teachers who do want to give a grade not to grade each bullet as a "present/absent" worth the same number of points because it may result in unfair grading. Consider a student who turned their camera off for 15 seconds while the teacher observed, but participated in the rest of the discussion. If the teacher grades each bullet as "present/absent" and as worth the same number of points, that 15-second camera break will result in a score of 87.5, which is not necessarily an accurate portrayal of the students' overall performance. Instead, the teacher may choose to deduct 5 points for the camera off, therefore, giving the student a 95, which may be more representative of these student's performance. Though we provide advice in this chapter for grading discussions, we always urge teachers to use their own professional judgment to make decisions that are *fair* and *representative of students' performance* rather than always adhering strictly to a set of specific rules.

Using Rubrics

Rubrics exist specifically for the purpose of grading elements that are naturally subjective in nature. This makes them challenging to use, and therefore increases the importance of using rubrics with well-defined criteria. It is also important to use rubrics not only as grading tools, but also as instructional tools (Brookhart, 2013). Rubrics are typically used to grade the quality, accuracy, and clarity of student responses. There is an art and science to creating strong rubrics, and readers should note that we are barely going to scratch the surface in this book. If readers are looking for more in-depth information on creating rubrics, we suggest Susan Brookhart's (2013) *How to Create and Use Rubrics for Formative Assessment and Grading* and Arter and McTighe's (2001) *Scoring Rubrics in the Classroom: Using Performance Criteria for Assessing and Improving Student Performance.*

There are two major choices to make when creating a rubric: (1) Do you want a holistic or an analytical rubric? and (2) Do you want a general or task-specific rubric?

> It is important to use rubrics not only as grading tools, but also as instructional tools

On a holistic rubric, the teacher gives a single, or holistic, score for the student response. The analytical rubric, on the other hand, breaks the criteria into categories, and the teacher provides a separate score for each category. Holistic rubrics tend to be faster to grade, but the downside is they may not always give specific criteria for each category to help students improve.

On a general rubric, the same rubric can be used for multiple tasks of the same type. This is useful because students can use the rubric over and over and master meeting the expectations. The downside, however, can be that tasks may vary slightly and the general rubric may not always fit perfectly. This is corrected through the use of a task-specific rubric. There are three main drawbacks for the task-specific rubric. First, students do not have the chance to become as familiar with them through multiple performances. Second, we said earlier that creating quality rubrics is an art and a science, and it can take a lot of work to create a quality rubric. Task specific rubrics also do not necessarily give the teacher the opportunity to refine the rubric over multiple performances. Lastly, if a teacher is frequently creating new rubrics, it can be hard for the teacher to internalize the components, therefore making grading take longer. In these next sections, we give recommendations for easy-use rubrics for both written and verbal discussions.

Rubrics for Written Discussions

Written discussions give students the opportunity to compose their thoughts more thoroughly before having to contribute a response (unless, of course, you are doing a real-time discussion over chat, in which case you may actually want to use the rubrics for verbal discussions). Our general recommendation for using rubrics with written discussions is that a teacher uses a very simple analytical rubric with the above criteria: quality, accuracy, and clarity. (We do not recommend grades younger than third use rubrics for written discussions; a checklist would be far more appropriate, but of course teachers should use their professional judgment). We also recommend using a general rubric for all discussions, rather than a task-specific rubric that changes from discussion to discussion. Below, you will see a sample rubric for written discussions. The rubric might seem overly complex at first glance, but we encourage teachers to pick and choose the categories that are most appropriate for the developmental levels of the students and best fit the content being used. For instance, if students are tasked with a discussion board discussing *To Kill a Mockingbird*, it may not be necessary for students to provide citations from sources. A teacher may also tweak the rubric wherever necessary. In a history class, for example, a teacher may also require that students use multiple sources in addition to quality sources, so we encourage the teacher to add that criteria to the rubric.

Sample Rubric for Written Discussions

	Needs Improvement	*Almost There*	*Excellent*
Quality	Answer is vague or does not address the parts of or all of the prompt	Answer mostly addresses the prompt	Answer thoroughly addresses the prompt
	Answer fails to address the success criteria in a meaningful way	Answer meets most of the assigned success criteria	Answer meets all assigned success criteria
	Point is either not supported by evidence, or no point is made	Makes a point and then backs it up with acceptable evidence	Makes a point and then backs it up with strong evidence
	Either does not respond to classmates or is disrespectful in either tone or response content	Responds to other classmates' with respectful answers	Responds to other classmates' with thoughtful and respectful answers
	Answer displays little creativity and/or is inappropriate for the task	Answer displays some creativity that is appropriate for the task	Answer displays creativity that is appropriate for the task and makes the answer interesting

	Needs Improvement	Almost There	Excellent
Accuracy	Answer demonstrates significant misconceptions	Almost all statements are factually true	All statements are factually true
	Several citations are missing and/or sources are not cited accurately and/or uses low quality sources	The majority of evidence is backed up by accurate citations from quality sources	All evidence is backed up by accurate citations from quality sources
Clarity	Follows all grammatical conventions but contains multiple errors and/or errors significantly detract from readability	Follows all grammatical conventions, but with errors that sometimes detract from readability	Follows all grammatical conventions, with no more than a few minor errors, and errors do not detract from readability

A note about this rubric: It is sometimes stated that rubrics should have four levels, and the rationale is usually that it keeps reviewers from marking everything in the middle column (when in doubt, people tend to gravitate toward away from extremes). We purposefully chose three levels for this rubric, however, as two might not provide enough gradation for performance levels, and four would start to be unwieldy for quick grading. Four or more levels might also be difficult for students to "keep in their minds" when responding. We believe that in the case of rubrics for discussions, three really is the magic number.

Rubrics for Verbal Discussions

Rubrics for verbal discussions present more of a challenge because a teacher is trying to listen and make judgments at the same time. Unlike written discussions, if we stop to ponder what grade to give a particular student, it's likely we will miss other key contributions to the discussion. For that reason, we recommend a much simpler rubric for verbal discussions than for written ones. While the rubric is technically an analytical one, in that it breaks the criteria into the three main categories, the rubric itself is more holistic in that the criteria for those categories is not broken apart like it is in the written discussion rubric. We again recommend teachers make professional judgments and tweak the rubric as necessary for the developmental needs of their students and to make it appropriate for the content.

Example Rubric for Verbal Discussions

Quality: Asks good questions, gives thoughtful answers, and participates neither too much nor too little	Rarely	Frequently	Almost Always
Accuracy: Statements are true	Rarely	Frequently	Almost Always
Clarity: Is easy to understand	Rarely	Frequently	Almost Always

Again the rubric has three levels, but this time teachers are giving frequency ratings. This is purposeful, in that it allows teachers to listen and grade quickly based on the holistic student performance.

Final Thoughts on Grading With Rubrics

If the teacher is using a rubric formatively, no grades and therefore points for criteria and levels are required. If the teacher wants to take a grade on a discussion, however, values must be assigned. Like we saw with the checklist, it might feel like logically, each component should be worth the same amount of points. The rubric, however, has multiple criteria under quality, and only one criteria under clarity. Clear responses are necessary for thriving discussions, however. For those reasons, we encourage teachers not to simply assign point values to the rubric based on the overall number of criteria, but to think deeply about the criteria they are using, and how important each is for the overall task ... and to then assign points or percentages for each rating accordingly. We also do not recommend that teachers neatly divide each rating by three (so that, for instance, excellent clarity would be worth 10 points, almost there is worth 5 points, and needs improvement is worth 0 points); the point difference between excellent and almost there should not necessarily be as great as the point difference between almost there and needs improvement. An example of how a teacher might assign grades will be seen in the Case Study example.

Virtual Discussion Strategies

Final Thoughts on Grading Discussions

The most important thing teachers can do when determining how to grade a discussion is to make sure the grading scheme makes sense for their students and the content being addressed. In some cases, that might be a combination of any of the rubrics above. For instance, teachers might require that students use a certain source in their written discussion responses. In that case, the student either uses the source or does not; the teacher can use a checkbox to grade that. On the other hand, the teacher may also want to grade the quality of ideas; in that case, the teacher might also use a simple three-level rubric. These kinds of decisions do take some deep thought, and that is one reason that we recommend using general rubrics for discussions rather than task specific. Generating a strong rubric takes time and consideration, and to do so for each individual discussion would be taxing on the teacher.

> The most important thing teachers can do is to make sure that the grading scheme makes sense for their students and the content

Case Study

Identify

Eamon Bennett teaches a virtual Algebra I class and is a firm believer in the importance of having students communicate clearly and frequently about their mathematical thinking. At least once a unit, he has students complete a multi-step problem that uses both current content and content from previous units. On the class discussion board, students must figure out their answer, explain the steps they took to solve the problem, and then discuss how efficient their methods were. They also need to upload a picture of their work. Students are required to read each other's answers, and then during the synchronous class time, they are put into breakout groups to discuss similarities and differences in the ways that group members attacked the problem, and, if they would do it over again, whether they would change their strategy.

Virtual Discussion Strategies

Plan

Mr. Bennett decides that he wants to include both some checklist items and some rubric items for the written discussions. He knows that in order to make the checklists and rubric work for mathematics, he needs to make some tweaks to the rubric for written discussions in this chapter. He also does not want the rubric to be overly long because he wants to be able to give students quick feedback. He, therefore, puts together the following checklist and rubric:

Correct Answer	☐ Yes *(5 points)*	☐ No *(0 points)*	
Uploaded completed work page	☐ Yes *(5 points)*	☐ No *(0 points)*	
	Needs Improvement	**Almost There**	**Excellent**
Quality	Includes only a few steps needed to solve the problem *(15 points)*	Includes most steps needed to solve the problem *(30 points)*	Includes all steps needed to solve the problem *(35 points)*
Accuracy	Uses few mathematical terms, forms, and/or other concepts, or demonstrates serious misconceptions *(15 points)*	Uses most mathematical terms, forms, and other concepts correctly *(30 points)*	Uses all mathematical terms, forms, and other concepts correctly *(35 points)*
Clarity	Follows all grammatical conventions but contains multiple errors and/or errors significantly detract from readability *(10 points)*	Follows all grammatical conventions, but with errors that sometimes detract from readability *(15 points)*	Follows all grammatical conventions, with no more than a few minor errors, and errors do not detract from readability *(20 points)*
TOTAL:		**GRADE:**	

Mr. Bennett purposefully made the weight of answer quality and mathematical term accuracy more important than actually getting the correct answer. Typically with mathematics problems, the focus is on the correct answer, but students do not necessarily know *how* they got that answer or *why* it is correct. To get a 100, of course the student would have to get the correct answer, but using a rubric likes this ensures that a student who understood the problem but simply made a small computational error (such as forgetting to regroup a ten), does not "fail" despite actually knowing how to solve the problem. What Mr. Bennett has found, however, is that students who score in the excellent or almost there categories tend to get the correct answer more often than not, because they are thinking through their work carefully.

For the verbal discussions, he decides that he wants to use a checklist because he feels like he can grade that more quickly, but he decides to use a hybrid of the verbal checklist and rubric, and therefore creates the following:

Quality:	YES NO
Asks good questions, gives thoughtful answers, and participates neither too much nor too little (0–45 points)	
Accuracy:	YES NO
Uses mathematical terms, formulas, and other concepts correctly (0–45 points)	
Clarity/Presentational:	YES NO
Speaks loudly and clearly enough to be understood (0–10 points)	
TOTAL	

Mr. Bennett decides that he will average the two grades together and use them as a quiz grade.

Apply

Mr. Bennett knows that the majority of his students may never have had to communicate their mathematical reasoning both verbally and in writing, so he decides that it is important to model to the students how to discuss mathematical concepts during a synchronous class session. For that reason, he starts with a simple multi-step problem. He asks students to simply write down in the chat box various steps they would take to solve the problem. They only send the messages to him, so that he can be sure that each student is providing a response rather than just copying the other students. He copies and pastes some of these responses onto a Google doc, sharing his screen with the students. He then walks students through how to create a paragraph using mathematical communications based on those answers. He assigns students a similar task for homework, reviews their paragraph, and provides general feedback.

The next week, Mr. Bennett gives students a similar multi-step problem, and has them asynchronously submit their paragraphs explaining the steps they took to solve the problem. He also completes a paragraph of his own, making some purposeful mistakes in it. He then displays the rubric to students and has a whole group discussion about how they would grade his paragraph. He then has students work in pairs to review and rewrite the paragraphs to make sure that they meet all the expectations on the rubric.

The following week, Mr. Bennett has students do the same task, but this time, they post their paragraphs on a discussion board. The discussion board has a feature that will not allow students to see others' work until they have submitted their own paragraphs first, so Mr. Bennett knows that the students' work is original. During the whole group, he and the students randomly choose two responses that both had the correct answer and then contrast how the students solved the problems. He shows students the rubric for the verbal discussions, and talks through the different criteria. Mr. Bennett then puts students into groups of three and has them compare and contrast how they solved the problems and wrote about it. Mr. Bennett visits each group and provides feedback to individuals as needed and then to the whole group after class. Students then do a self-rating with the verbal rubric.

Assess

Finally, Mr. Bennett is ready to have the students engage in the actual task. He assigns the students a multi-step problem and has them solve it, upload their work, and then write a paragraph explaining how they solved it. He grades students using the written discussion rubric and allows students to fix any mistakes before the next class (if they do, he will regrade). During that next class, he puts students into groups of three and has them discuss with one another, while he visits each breakout group and grades students with the verbal discussion rubric.

Refine

After reviewing how his students did, Mr. Bennett realizes that only 55% of students scored an excellent in the quality criteria ("Includes all steps needed to solve the problem") on the written discussion rubric. Most students left out one or more steps that they used when solving the problem. Mr. Bennett talks to students and asks how they wrote their paragraphs; most students explained that they solved the problem computationally, and then went back and wrote the paragraph. Mr. Bennett asks students to reverse the order, so that students write the paragraph with the steps first, and then follow each of their written steps to get the answer, and then demonstrates to students how to do this. He gives the students a similar task the next week, and the number of students scoring an excellent in the quality criteria goes up to 80%.

In the verbal discussions, he found that only 35% of students scored the full 20 points in the quality criterion ("Asks good questions, gives thoughtful answers, and participates neither too much nor too little"). He noticed during his observations that students knew how to explain their own thinking, but were not good at asking each other questions. He therefore does a model lesson on how to ask rich questions in a mathematical class, and provides students with a list of question starters. He puts students in pairs and has one person explain their thinking while the other person does nothing but ask questions, and then they switch. The next week when he does a similar task again, students are allowed to use their prompts and he finds that the number of students who score the full 20 points for the quality criterion goes up to 65%.

Professional Development Plan for This Chapter

1. Bring together your teacher teams either in a full meeting or in the smaller professional learning community groups.
2. Select one teacher who will share about a lesson they will facilitate within the next week or two and ask them to provide a summary of the lesson, with a focus on the types of virtual discussion activities and strategies they will use. It is suggested that the teachers in the

session receive a copy of the lesson plan in advance and the team reviews the discussion activities and explores the technology tools being used for the lesson.

a. Teacher presents for up to 10 minutes, focusing on the discussion activities and strategies.
b. 5 minutes: thought partners describe what they heard and share about how they feel the activity will be perceived by students and how students will engage in the activity. If time permits, describe the level of engagement (see Chapter 2).
c. Presenting teacher reflects back what they heard and discusses if they will make revisions to the lessons based on the feedback.
d. Continue activity with the remaining group members.

Virtual Tools for This Strategy at Time of Publication

Capabilities	Kialo Edu	Padlet	Backchannel Chat	Flipgrid	Yo Teach!
Supports text discussions	✔	✔	✔	✔	✔
Supports audio or audio/video discussions		A/V can be linked but no built-in recording is available	A/V can be linked but no built-in recording is available	✔	
Supports teacher moderation of discussions	✔	✔	✔	✔	
Supports grouping students for differentiation	✔	✔	✔	✔	✔
Allows private teacher feedback for students	✔	If a Padlet is restricted to one student	✔	✔	
Payment level	Free	Free/Moderate	Free/Minimal	Free	Free

Quick Comparison

Kialo Edu is an online discussion tool designed to facilitate debates over ideas. Teachers or students can post claims or prompts, and then students respond in text form with pros, cons, evidence, commentary, and more. Arguments are tracked and illustrated with auto-generating graphics in interactive tree structures, and student engagement with ideas is also illustrated. Teachers can create different prompts for different groups of students, allowing for differentiation. Discussions are only available to the specific students with which the teacher shares the content and are unavailable to others. Teachers can also assign different roles for students—Editor, Writer, or Viewer, for example—which can be useful in scaffolding individual student responsibility as their discussion skills grow over time.

Padlet, as discussed in a previous chapter, is an online collaboration tool that allows users to interact with each other's ideas using text, images, video, and more. This makes Padlet a quick and easy discussion tool that requires minimal effort to get up and running. Unlike *Kialo Edu*, it does not do advanced illustrations of arguments, but it does feature several comment organization display styles.

Backchannel Chat is a chat room-based tool for discussions. Teachers can post prompts and students can respond in real-time. Teachers can turn on comment moderation if desired. Multimedia elements can be embedded to further liven the discussions. The free version provides limited use, but the inexpensive paid version adds file sharing, private messaging between individual students and the teacher, integrations with some learning management systems, and the ability to generate contribution lists by student—great for supporting assessment.

Flipgrid was also discussed in a previous chapter. Originally designed as a video-discussion tool, *Flipgrid* now also supports text discussions via its Comments feature. Text-based comments can be moderated by the teacher, and groups can be created so that students have specific peers with which to interact. Entire discussions can take place via text rather than through video—video need not be required for students to participate. This is an important factor for situations where displaying a student's home in the background of their video may be a sensitive issue.

Yo Teach! is another chat room-based tool for discussions. Teachers can create rooms and then post discussion prompts; students join rooms using the URL and the room password. Much like regular chat rooms, *Yo Teach!* discussions are free-flowing live streams with no structure. Discussions will proceed as quickly or as slowly as the students type comments. Discussions can be exported for later review and evaluation. Additionally, an integrated whiteboard feature allows for limited non-text commentary. While teachers can remove comments and can mute or remove students from a room, comments cannot be moderated before they appear to all participants. There is no authentication of participants—students do not have accounts—and so teachers must take care to ensure their students are mature enough to use the tool respectfully.

Notes

1. To muddy the waters a bit, checklists are actually a type of rubric. They are the most basic form of a rubric, because the criteria are either present or not; a checklist is, essentially, a rubric with only two levels. For the clarity purposes in this chapter, however, we will use the terms "checklist" and "rubric" as separate entities.

2. We acknowledge that some people might say this is more of a "rating scale" than a rubric. Like the checklist is a rubric with only two levels, however, we believe that a rating scale is also a type rubric. Understanding that all of these things are "rubrics" helps keep us from feeling like we must follow rules of one type or another, and instead allows us to design the grading scheme that makes the most sense.

References

Anderman, E. M. (2002). School effects on psychological outcomes during adolescence. *Journal of Educational Psychology, 94*(4), 795.

Arter, J., & McTighe, J. (2001). *Scoring rubrics in the classroom: Using performance criteria for assessing and improving student performance.* Corwin.

Brookhart, S. M. (2013). *How to create and use rubrics for formative assessment and grading*. ASCD.

Burhan, R., & Moradzadeh, J. (2020). Neurotransmitter dopamine (DA) and its role in the development of social media addiction. *Journal of Neurology & Neurophysiology, 11*(7), 1–2.

D'Arienzo, M. C., Boursier, V., & Griffiths, M. D. (2019). Addiction to social media and attachment styles: A systematic literature review. *International Journal of Mental Health and Addiction, 17*(4), 1094–1118.

Finn, J. D. (1989). Withdrawing from school. *Review of Educational Research, 59*(2), 117–142.

Hattie, J. (2003). Teachers make a difference, What is the research evidence?

Hattie, J., & Yates, G. C. (2013). *Visible learning and the science of how we learn*. Routledge.

Johnson, L. S. (2009). School contexts and student belonging: A mixed methods study of an innovative high school. *School Community Journal, 19*(1), 99–118.

Osterman, K. F. (2000). Students' need for belonging in the school community. *Review of Educational Research, 70*(3), 323–367.

Virtual Performance Strategies

Translating live performances to virtual experiences can be one of the biggest challenges in online classrooms. But it is possible! Too often we hear from brick and mortar teachers that courses such as drama and physical education cannot be taught online ... but we also know plenty of teachers who make a living by teaching just those kinds of courses in online environments. It is true teachers must be especially thoughtful when creating and grading these types of performances in a virtual environment. Types of performances may include musical performances (e.g., dance, singing, playing an instrument), dramatic performances (monologues, dialogues, or plays with multiple characters), or performing simple tasks (e.g., grouping and regrouping with base ten-blocks, dribbling a basketball). Not teaching in-person means students will need to perform the task on camera, whether live or recorded. Recorded performances, of course, add the complicating factor of requiring students to learn extra recording software, how to upload these videos to the virtual classroom, and potentially how to edit them. This first section of this chapter will discuss how to create virtual performance assessments by writing clear prompts, teach necessary skills beforehand, model successful performances, and, if students are presenting to one another, determine the task they will accomplish while watching classmates. The grading section of this chapter describes determining whether students get to do "retakes," and how to use rubrics for online performances, and other best practices for grading performances. Lastly, a case study example of using performances in the social studies classroom will be presented.

Creating Virtual Performance Assignments

Teachers who teach performance-heavy subjects in-person frequently have more leeway to change their approach quickly if needed, whereas the format of virtual teaching may make this more difficult. To change a performance task, students may have to gather new materials, learn new technologies, and find new places to do their performance. For these reasons, it is important that teachers carefully map out the performance beforehand.

Writing Clear Prompts

Writing clear prompts for any assignment is a good idea, but it is essential for an assessment on a student performance. Students need to know exactly what is required by them ahead of time in order to create a plan to complete the project. In cases where adults may be helping students at home (especially younger students), the teacher may be writing the prompt as much for the adults as for the student. The teacher, therefore, needs to outline any skills students will need to be taught beforehand and any materials that will be needed, which is another reason a clear prompt is crucial. For instance, consider the following prompts for various subject areas.

Drama	a. Students will present a monologue.
	b. Students will memorize and present a comedic monologue to the class. The monologue should be 2–3 minutes and performed while seated.
Music	a. Students will play a scale.
	b. Students will be randomly asked to play two of the following scales: either C-Major or G-major; and either A-major or F-major.
Mathematics	a. Students count a random collection.
	b. Students will count a random number of paperclips, between 10 and 50, by lining them up in groups of 10s. Students will count them by 1s and then also by 10s.
Science	a. Students will conduct a science experiment.
	b. Students will conduct a science experiment in which they test three different designs of paper airplanes in order to determine, which can fly the farthest.

(Continued)

Virtual Performance Strategies

(Continued)

History
a. Students will participate in a debate.
b. Students will participate in a debate as either a Patriot or a Loyalist, explaining why they believe various Acts of Parliament prior to the American Revolution were just or unjust. Students will be paired in groups of four (two per side) and each group will be given a random act to debate (Townshend Acts, the Tea Act, the Stamp Act, the Quartering Act). Each side will have 10 minutes to prepare their 1-minute opening statements; each person must speak for 30 seconds). Each side will then have 10 minutes to prepare their 2-minute rebuttals to the opening statements (each person must speak for 1 minute), and then 10 minutes to prepare their 1-minute closing statements (30 seconds per person).

Depending on the task, students may need more or less information. One way teachers can check their prompts for anything missing is to show the prompt to a colleague and

> Teachers should remain open to amending the prompts as students ask questions

ask the question, "What else would you need to know to successfully complete this assignment?" Teachers can also ask their students the same question, and then rebuild the prompt as students ask their questions. Note that students may need time to digest the prompt before being able to describe what else they need to know. It may even be that students have to begin working on the performance before they realize what questions they have, and the teacher should remain open to amending the prompt as these questions are asked and answered. In fact, if this is the first time a teacher is using a particular prompt, it may even be good practice to tell students up front the prompt may become more explicit as questions are asked by students and the teacher provides answers.

Determining What Materials and Skills Students Need Beforehand

One challenge of the virtual instruction is that it can be more difficult to give students the necessary materials for them to complete their performances. Not all performances require materials, of course, but many do. For instance, it is obviously impossible to know if a child can play the C-major scale on a

Virtual Performance Strategies

trombone if that child does not have a trombone. There can also be equity concerns, as some students may have more access to materials at home than others. For instance, if asking students to write and read a monologue from the point of view of a famous American, the teacher should not offer extra points for costumes or props unless those are somehow being provided to students.

For these reasons, teachers need to carefully think through the required materials for a performance. If the virtual program is one in which students are allowed to pick and choose their classes, then it is more acceptable for teachers to require a wider variety of materials; students have the choice not to sign up for a class if they do not have the appropriate materials. But if the virtual program requires students to take certain classes, it is important to limit the number of materials students are required to use to complete assignments. For these reasons, we recommend teachers to stick to one of the following: (1) performances that require no special materials; (2) performances that can be completed with free online resources; (3) performances that use common household items; or (4) performances that will be completed with materials that will be provided to the students.

Additionally, teachers need to consider whether students must be taught to use specific technology before completing their performances. For instance, if students will need to record themselves, then they may need to be taught to use a recording software such as Flipgrid. Flipgrid is a free online video recording software that is relatively intuitive to use, but if students will be using any of the features beyond simply pressing the Record button, it is crucial a teacher teaches these skills beforehand. Otherwise, the teacher may actually be grading the student's previous technology experience and/or whether there is someone at home to help students. It may be tempting to let older students "figure it out," but we have noticed that even when working with graduate students at the collegiate level, a minimal amount of training goes a long way toward decreasing anxiety and allowing students to focus on the task at hand, rather than trying to complete the task while fumbling through the technology.

> If students will be using any of the features beyond simply pressing the Record button, it is crucial to teach these skills beforehand

For younger students, teachers may even need to train *parents or guardians* on how to use the necessary technology. It may be possible for a teacher to meet synchronously

Virtual Performance Strategies

with parents to teach them, but if not, the teacher will include either videos or tipsheets geared toward adults that explain, step-by-step, how to help the student accomplish the task. If working with pre-readers, it is helpful to have two separate sets of videos and/or tipsheets. While the first set should include directions for an adult helping the child, the second should be a simple step-by-step guide for students that uses mostly pictures and/or simple words. This way, the adult can work with the child for the first few times, and then the child can use the simple instructions afterward to remind him or her of the steps. In this way, teachers are not only teaching students the content, but valuable technology skills that may well help them later in life.

Determining Tasks for Students as Audience Members

Too frequently we see classrooms where students perform for one another while the rest of the students play the role of bored audience members. It may sound harsh,

> Students anxiously await their own turn, and tune out as everyone else then performs

but watching young people perform skills they have just learned is usually not particularly entertaining in and of itself. If you're a parent and you've been to a children's recital, you may have experienced this phenomenon: you are riveted when it's your child and, at best, politely disinterested when watching other people's kids. Believe it or not, students feel the same way. They sit and anxiously await their own turn, and then tune out as everyone else performs.

While bored students are less of a behavior problem online (because teachers can just mute them or turn off their cameras if these students start to provide their own entertainment), some of the more enterprising young people may even be tempted to add humor to their performance where inappropriate, simply to amuse their classmates, preferring social capital over a grade. Additionally, bored audience members are more likely to simply wander away from their device or furtively use a second device to entertain themselves.

For all these reasons, we recommend that teachers do one of the following: (1) have students pre-record presentations that the teacher watches without students present; (2) have students perform just for the teacher; or (3) provide students who are watching with a list of things to look for during presentations, and then provide feedback to one another based on this list. Let's first look at point (1) where students have pre-recorded presentations that the teacher watches without students present. When a teacher chooses this model, students can still watch each other's presentations and provide feedback to one another as long as the videos are accessible to all and the teacher sets up a way for feedback to be provided. Some software programs have this kind of functionality built-in, such as Flipgrid, which easily allows students to record responses to one another if the teacher enables that setting. The teacher can also utilize a discussion board format that allows students to post links to their videos (which can be uploaded to sites such as Google Drive, YouTube, or Vimeo) and then respond to each other with feedback. If using this method, we do recommend that the teacher limit the length of the pre-recorded video or only require students to respond to a handful of videos. Limiting the number of responses in such a manner ensures that students do not become fatigued while trying to get through hours of video, therefore, impacting the effectiveness of their feedback.

Some tasks, however, are meant only for the eyes of the teacher. For instance, a teacher may want to see students count a number of objects and arrange them into groups of ten. If students watch each other while completing this task, the students who go last have an unfair advantage because they have had the chance to watch several other students complete the task. In another example, a band teacher may want students to sight-read a piece of music. Allowing students to hear others play, it is once again unfair for those students who go first. Of course, the teacher could choose a different piece of music for all students, but it might be time consuming to find all those different pieces, and might ultimately impact the validity of the task itself by comparing apples to oranges. Teachers can either set up a specific time for students to log on individually to perform the piece, or they can take individual students into a breakout room to complete the performance while the other students complete a classwork assignment. If a teacher chooses the latter, we recommend that the classwork assignment be one that students can easily complete independently so they do not need the teacher's help. Between each student, the teacher should check back in with the group and see if there are any questions from the students completing the independent

Virtual Performance Strategies

assignment. Unless students are particularly trustworthy, we also recommend that teachers ensure that the main group of students is muted and can only message the teacher, rather than each other. The teacher may also want to have students turn off their cameras to ensure that nothing untoward happens while the teacher is not in the main room.

In the last option for this section, the teacher provides students who are viewing others' presentations with a list of things to look for during presentations so students can provide feedback to one another. There are several considerations to ensure that this method is actually useful to both the student performers and the student audience members. First, we only recommend this approach if students' presentations are unique from one another. Having students watch each other sing scales or dribble a basketball over and over will not be particularly riveting, and student attention will most likely wander and therefore decrease the value of the provided feedback. Second, we recommend that students provide qualitative feedback in addition to any quantitative feedback, i.e., they should discuss the strengths and opportunities for growth in the presentations they are watching. Not only does this provide more ideas to the student performers, it also helps the student audience members think more deeply about the performance, and makes it more likely that their attention will be sustained. Next, we recommend that the teacher model how to complete this kind of feedback with students beforehand, and give students opportunities to practice how to give kind, thoughtful, and helpful feedback to one another (see also the THINK strategy from Chapter 3). Lastly, if at all possible, we recommend that all students do not perform on the same day, but rather that presentations are spread out, to the greatest extent possible, over multiple days. This can also help students in the audience sustain attention for their peers.

If a teacher chooses to let students provide feedback for one another, we recommend that prior to presentations, students are given a copy of the success criteria, rubric, checklist, or anything else that will be used to determine student achievement. The teacher may need to reword some of the language,

> Give students opportunities to practice how to give kind, thoughtful, and helpful feedback to one another

depending on the developmental level of the students. We do not recommend that students provide "grades" to one another, but rather that feedback between students be kept formative. In addition to having students refer to the criteria, rubrics, or checklist, it may be helpful for teachers to have students give their feedback using one of the following protocols. Note that these protocols can also be added to a form to collect students' typed responses to give to the group. If using this method, we do recommend that the teacher skim the responses before sending them on to presenters.

Glows	Grows
What worked well	*Opportunities for Improvement*

I Love...	I Wonder...
What worked well	*Opportunities for Improvement or Questions*

+	△
Definitely Keep!	*Consider tweaking...*

Green Light	Red Light	Yellow Light
This was great!	*Consider changing...*	*Questions*

Grading Virtual Performance Assignments

Teachers frequently choose to use performance assessments for formative purposes only. For instance, a teacher may ask a kindergarten student to recite their ABCs, identify sight words, or read a short passage, not to assign a grade, but rather to determine the next instructional steps for the student. Even if a grade is not assigned, we still suggest that a teacher determine the criteria for success ahead of time. For instance, if a student forgets a letter and must be prompted, does that count as a "successful attempt?" Are students allowed to "self-correct" or attempt to sound out sight words? How many words per minute must a student read to be considered "fluent?" It can be easy not to think about these questions until the assessment is already underway, and even with careful forethought, a teacher still may find it necessary to revamp the grading criteria during or after the assessment takes place. The next section helps teachers plan their grading procedures ahead of time by looking at whether the teacher will allow redos, how to use rubrics or rating scales to grade student performance, and by outlining other best practices in grading performances.

To Allow or Not to Allow "Redos"

There are many reasons to allow students to redo their performances. For instance, if a student is learning to play or sing a particular piece of music, the student *should* be practicing over and over until they nail the performance. Likewise, if a Digital Studio teacher wants to see that students can manipulate editing software, the student should be allowed to engage in "practice takes" until they can complete the task fluidly. A drama teacher may want students to concentrate more on tone and inflection during a monologue performance, rather than being able to do the performance from memory, and may similarly be fine with students recording and re-recording their performances.

On the other hand, teachers may also decide that it does not make sense to allow students to redo a less-than-stellar performance. If a physical education teacher is watching a student do pull-ups, the first performance is likely to be the same as the fifteenth performance (unless the student has a dramatic amount of time between performances to put on muscle). A drama teacher *might* want to see how students perform live, just as a music teacher might want to assess student sight-reading performances. A government teacher might need to see how a student will do in a live debate, just as a mathematics teacher may want to see how a student will attack an unfamiliar word problem.

Therefore, when deciding whether students should be allowed to redo performances, we recommend that teachers use the following table:

Consider allowing redos when...	Consider not allowing redos when...
❏ Students are recording performances for the teacher or other students to watch at a later date	❏ Students are performing live with other students as the audience
❏ Performances are for summative grades at the end of a unit or course	❏ The performance is purely for formative purposes to determine the students' current skill level in order to make instructional decisions
❏ Performances are of a rote skill or action that students should be able to perform fluidly; students can and should be practicing beforehand	❏ Performances are on new or unfamiliar material to see how students handle it (i.e., a cold reading passage, sight reading, etc.); students cannot really practice
❏ The students' performance level is likely to change in a short amount of time if the student practices	❏ The students' performance level is unlikely to change in a short amount of time even if the student practices

As always, we recommend that teachers use their professional judgment. The teacher may find the current performance assignment has some check marks under the "Consider allowing redos" category and the "Consider not allowing redos" category. When this happens, the teacher can determine whether to go with allowing no redos, unlimited redos, or limited redos. For instance, if a student is performing in real-time (rather than in a recording) by counting number cubes and gets mixed up halfway through, the teacher may say that the student can restart up to two times. For longer performances, such as playing a longer piece of music, the teacher may tell students that they can start over from a certain point, rather than going all the way back to the beginning. The teacher should also use professional judgment to determine whether to let students know ahead of time that they will be allowed a certain number of redos. As we will discuss in the next section, the teacher may also decide to include whether the student needed to start over as a part of the grade.

Using Rubrics to Grade Performances

It is possible to use checklists to grade a performance, and may even be appropriate in some cases. However, we recommend that teachers use rubrics (including rating scales, which are a type of rubric) because most performance grades require that the teacher judge the quality of students' performances. Therefore, this section will be dedicated to using rubrics

Virtual Performance Strategies

for grading performances. If a teacher is interested in using a checklist, check out the Chapter 3 section on checklists (even though Chapter 3 is specifically on using and grading discussions,

> We recommend rubrics because most performance grades require that the teacher judge the quality of students' performances

the main ideas about checklists can apply to any task).

Additionally, a teacher must decide beforehand whether to share the rubric with students. This works well if the teacher is having students record their performances and allowing unlimited redos, because students can continue to refine their performance until they meet or exceed the criteria. On the other hand, if students are performing live, knowing the rubric ahead of time may make students more nervous as they try to both perform and keep the rubric in their heads. A teacher can also take a middle approach by telling students what the categories on the rubric will be, so that students know to concentrate on those aspects, without showing the students the entire rubric.

Determining Rubric Categories

The three aspects that a rubric for performances will usually grade are quality, accuracy, and clarity, though not all of these will be used for every performance. Therefore, the

> A rubric for performances will usually grade quality, accuracy, and clarity

first thing the teacher needs to do when finding, tweaking, or creating a rubric is to determine the most important aspects of the performance. For instance, is memorization a key point of the performance...or is this a performance in which students must apply their skills to an unfamiliar situation (e.g., an unfamiliar reading passage, sight reading, a new debate topic, etc.)? Is there key content that must be included in the performance, or is the performance completely skill based?

Once the teacher has decided which of the performance aspects (quality, accuracy, clarity) are most important, we then recommend that the teacher consider what that quality, accuracy, and/or clarity would look like

Virtual Performance Strategies

if performed at the highest level. Let's look back at some of the previous performance prompts and consider what aspects may be most important for grading each, and how a teacher might conceptualize the highest level of performance.

Drama	Students will memorize and present a comedic monologue to the class. The monologue should be 2–3 minutes and performed while seated.	→ Quality (Were the tone, facial expressions, etc., appropriate for the monologue?) → Accuracy (Was the monologue appropriately memorized?) → Clarity (Was the monologue performed at an appropriate pace and volume so as to be easily understood?)
Music	Students will be randomly asked to play two of the following scales: either C-Major or G-major; and, either A-major or F-major.	→ Quality (What was the quality of the instrument's tone?) → Accuracy (Was the scale played with minimal or no mistakes?)
Mathematics	Students will count a random number of paperclips, between 10 and 50, by lining them up in groups of 10s. Students will count them by 1s and then also by 10s.	→ Accuracy (Did students count correctly with few or no mistakes and without prompting?)
Science	Students will conduct a science experiment in which they test three different designs of paper airplanes in order to determine which can fly the farthest.	→ Quality (Did the student perform an experiment that included all aspects of the scientific method in a way that could be replicated?) → Accuracy (Were the data collection, analysis, and conclusions completed accurately?) → Clarity (Were procedures and conclusions clear and was data presented in a clear way that was easy to understand?)

(*Continued*)

(Continued)

History	Students will participate in a debate as either a Patriot or a Loyalist, explaining why they believe various Acts of Parliament prior to the American Revolution were just or unjust. Students will be paired in groups of four (two per side) and each group will be given a random act to debate (Townshend Acts, the Tea Act, the Stamp Act, the Quartering Act). Each side will have 10 minutes to prepare their 1-minute opening statements; each person must speak for 30 seconds). Each side will then have 10 minutes to prepare their 2-minute rebuttals to the opening statements (each person must speak for 1 minute), and then 10 minutes to prepare their 1-minute closing statements (30 seconds per person).	→ Quality (Did each student include relevant historical information to justify their claims? Did they address counterclaims productively?) → Accuracy (Were included historical facts correct and any interpretations of these facts free of misconception?) → Clarity (Did students speak at a pace and volume that was easily understood?)

It can be difficult to determine how many categories are necessary, and the first time that a teacher uses a particular performance task with students, the teacher may find that they include too many or too few categories. There is no "correct" number of categories; for some performances, a single category may be sufficient. For longer or more complex performances, more categories may be required. Individual teachers may also find they have more or less patience for grading a long-list of categories. In the end, there should be enough categories so that students can receive sufficient feedback about their performances, but not so many that categories are too similar and/or the rubric becomes overwhelming for both the teacher and the student.

Determining Rubric Levels

Similar to the number of categories, we generally recommend having as few performance levels as possible in a way that still provides the students with the feedback they need to improve. If the performance is being used for a summative grade, we also recommend having the fewest number of levels needed for the teacher to determine a grade that is best indicative of the performance.

For a performance that is being used purely for formative purposes, a teacher may want to consider a single-point rubric. The single-point rubric is one of the easiest for a teacher to create and grade and for students to understand. To create a single point rubric, the teacher first needs to determine the categories and then simply describe a successful performance for each of the categories. These get listed down the middle of the rubric, and then on either side, the teacher writes comments on how the student either met/exceeded or did not meet the performance criteria.

Let's consider the Drama monologue assignment from above: "Students will memorize and present a comedic monologue to the class. The monologue should be 2–3 minutes and performed while seated." When converted to a single point rubric, it might look like this:

Grows	Criteria	Glows
	→ **Quality:** The student's tone, facial expressions, and body language were appropriate for the monologue. → **Accuracy:** The student memorized the monologue and performed without any mistakes that distracted from the performance. → **Clarity:** The student performed the monologue at an appropriate pace and volume, and could therefore be easily understood.	

While the single point rubric is easy to use for formative purposes, it does present more of a challenge if giving a summative grade, especially if there are relatively few categories and the teacher is grading on a 100 point scale. For instance, in the above rubric, a teacher might assign the quality category as 35 points, the accuracy category as 30 points, and the clarity category as 35 points. If each category has a range of over 30 points, it can be difficult for

Virtual Performance Strategies

a teacher to assign fair grades consistently. That is, after all, the main purpose of a rubric: To allow teachers to provide grades that are subject to professional opinion but with a consistency that makes it fair to students.

For that reason, if a teacher intends to use performance summatively to provide a grade, we recommend that the teacher use a more detailed rubric that adequately reflects the complexity involved in awarding grades fairly and consistently. The goal, however, is to make rubric exactly as complex as it needs to be, without making it any more so. This can be a tricky thing to do, and teachers may find that they need to tweak their rubrics, especially if using them for the first time.

While there is no hard and fast rule regarding the number of rubric levels, many rubrics tend to gravitate toward four levels. Four levels provide enough differentiation without becoming overly difficult to distinguish differences between levels. As always, however, the teacher should use professional judgment and make changes to rubrics as necessary after implementing them.

As an example of a more complex rubric, let's look again at the social studies performance prompt:

History	Students will participate in a debate as either a Patriot or a Loyalist, explaining why they believe various Acts of Parliament prior to the American Revolution were just or unjust. Students will be paired in groups of four (two per side) and each group will be given a random act to debate (Townshend Acts, the Tea Act, the Stamp Act, the Quartering Act). Each side will have 10 minutes to prepare their 1-minute opening statements; each person must speak for 30 seconds). Each side will then have 10 minutes to prepare their 2-minute rebuttals to the opening statements (each person must speak for 1 minute), and then 10 minutes to prepare their 1-minute closing statements (30 seconds per person).	→ Quality (Did each student include relevant historical information to justify their claims? Did they address counterclaims productively?) → Accuracy (Were included historical facts correct and any interpretations of these facts free of misconception?) → Clarity (Did students speak at a pace and volume that was easily understood?)

This rubric again has three categories: quality, accuracy, and clarity. We can grade each of these holistically (i.e., give one overall grade for quality, one for accuracy, and one for clarity), or we can break these categories down into the questions that you see above under each category. There is no right or wrong way to do this, but for the sake of example, we will choose to break up the categories into questions, therefore, giving us two criteria for quality, and one each for accuracy and clarity. We will choose to weigh each criteria equally, therefore, making quality worth 50% of the overall grade, with accuracy and consistency each being worth 25%. Then, we will create four levels for each criteria, so that our rubric looks like this:

Criteria	Needs Improvement (0–14 points)	Getting There (15 points)	Almost! (20 points)	Great job! (25 points)
Quality	Includes little or no relevant historical information to justify claims	Justifies some of the claims with historical information	Justifies the majority of claims with historical information	Justifies all claims with a wide variety of relevant historical information
	Addresses few or no counterclaims, and/or none productively	Addresses some counterclaims productively	Addresses most counterclaims productively	Addresses all counterclaims productively
Accuracy	Includes historical information that demonstrates major inaccuracies or misconceptions	Includes historical information that demonstrates moderate inaccuracies or misconceptions	Includes mostly accurate historical information, with minor inaccuracies and few or no misconceptions	Includes a variety of historical information, all of which is accurate and free of misconception
Clarity	Spoke with a pace and/or volume that were very difficult to understand	Spoke with a pace and/or volume that were difficult to understand at times	Spoke with a pace and/or volume that were almost always understood	Spoke with a pace and/or volume that were easily understood

In this rubric, we choose to make the highest level the one that meets all the expectations, but it is also appropriate to make the highest level one that exceeds expectations. A rubric that makes the highest level one that exceeds expectations assumes a bell curve, with most students scoring proficient (usually in the 75–90% range) with a few students scoring in the exceeding expectation range (usually 90–100%). The rubric above takes a mastery approach, assuming that all students can (and maybe should) meet the given expectations if properly prepared. The teacher will need to consider which underlying philosophy makes the most sense for the students' developmental levels, the content, and the particular task.

In the above example, we also gave specific point values for each level. "Great Job!" was worth 25 points, "Almost!" was worth 20 points, etc ... Giving a specific point value for each level increases consistency between grades, but it does cut down on the amount of professional judgment a teacher can use, and may prove difficult when a student performs between levels. It is also, therefore, appropriate to use a grading structure like this:

Criteria	Needs Improvement (0–12 points)	Getting There (13–17 points)	Almost! (18–22 points)	Great job! (23–25 points)

The mean point value for each level is close to the definitive point values in the previous example. Again, there are no correct ways to break up points for each level; there are only methods that are more or less appropriate for the task at hand. When creating or tweaking a rubric, it can be helpful for the teacher to justify their grading scheme to another professional to make sure that the underlying logics and assumptions match the task expectations.

Best Practices in Grading Recorded Performances

Grading recorded performances, especially those longer than about 3 minutes, can be tiring for teachers. For that reason, we share some "best practices" when grading these types of performances:

1. **Watch a handful of performances before grading.** Choose students you think will most likely score low, average, and high. Test out your rubric by grading these students. Do the scores that you get when using your rubric align with your perception of how well students met the requirements? If not, your rubric may need tweaking.
2. **Don't grade all at once if performances are long.** Fatigue can lead to inconsistent grading. It's better to spread out the grading if possible, while of course also trying to return grades or feedback in a timely manner. Even if grading all performances in a day or two, take short brain breaks after every three or four performances.
3. **Release grades all at once.** This is especially important if you are using a rubric for the first time. You might realize after a handful of performances that you need to edit your rubric and potentially go back and change previous grades as appropriate. You don't want to do this after students have already seen their grades.
4. **Provide both quantitative and qualitative feedback.** While a rubric like the one we used for the history debate provides a decent amount of qualitative feedback on its own, we recommend still providing specifics to students regarding why they did or did not meet expectations, including how they can continue to improve their performance.

Case Study

Identify

Ashanti Morris teaches a high school business class for seniors. One of the tasks in her curriculum is to have students participate in a mock interview for a job in a business field. Each interview lasts 15 minutes and includes a committee that consists of Ms. Morris and two local business leaders. At the end of the interview, the interview committee gives feedback to each interviewee.

Plan

Ms. Morris knows that in order to give consistent feedback, she needs a rubric that can be easily understood by both students and interviewers. She plans to go through the rubric with students, show them videos of example interviews and works through how she would evaluate them, and then have the students practice with each other. The rubric, therefore, needs to be detailed enough to allow for inter- and intrarater reliability, but simple enough that it can easily be used during interviews with a quick turnaround. She knows that it also needs to be free of educational jargon.

Ms. Morris decides that she will include two main categories: quality and clarity. She knows that accuracy is also important, but this is a general business class, and the interviewers will come from various business backgrounds, and therefore may not be able to judge the technical accuracy of jobs for which students may apply. Ms. Morris decides that the following questions should be answerable at the end of each interview:

1. Did the student fully answer each part of each question?
2. Did students' answers show examples of their workplace skills and ethics (punctuality, integrity, perseverance, etc.)?
3. Did students' answers show examples of critical thinking, creativity, and the ability to collaborate effectively?
4. Did students exhibit professional dress?
5. Did students maintain good posture and appropriate camera angle and lighting?
6. Did students speak clearly (volume, pace, etc.)?
7. Did students use business-appropriate language?

While Ms. Morris decides not to categorize these categories as "Quality" or "Clarity" on the rubric itself, she notes to herself that Questions 1–5 tend to focus on quality, whereas Questions 6 and 7 focus on clarity. That being said, she thinks that Questions 1–3 work best under the main category of "Quality of Answers" and Questions 4–7 under the main category of "Presentation Skills." She decides to have four levels.

	Improvement Needed	Wish You the Best, But No Thanks	Considered for a Position	Definitely Hired
		Quality of Answers		
Answer Completeness	Frequently misses major parts of questions, answers don't fit questions, or rambles frequently (0–4 points)	Answers some parts of questions, but needs some redirection and/or rambles at times (6 points)	Answers most parts of most questions; rambles minimally (8 points)	Fully answers each part of each question without rambling (10 points)
Workplace Skills	Gives answers that demonstrate a lack of responsibility, integrity, and perseverance (0–9 points)	Gives answers that demonstrate uneven levels of responsibility, integrity, and perseverance (10 points)	Gives answers that demonstrate adequate levels of responsibility, integrity, and perseverance (15 points)	Gives answers that demonstrate high levels of responsibility, integrity, and perseverance (20 points)
Problem-Solving Skills	Gives answers that demonstrate a lack of creativity and critical thinking, and/or the ability to work with others to solve problems (0–9 points)	Answers demonstrate uneven levels of creativity and critical thinking, and the ability to work with others to solve problems (10 points)	Answers demonstrate adequate levels of creativity and critical thinking, and the ability to work with others to solve problems (15 points)	Answers demonstrate high levels of creativity and critical thinking, and the ability to work with others to solve problems (20 points)

(Continued)

Virtual Performance Strategies

(Continued)

	Improvement Needed	Wish You the Best, But No Thanks	Considered for a Position	Definitely Hired
Presentation Skills				
Professional Dress[1]	Wears clothes that have excessive rips, stains, wrinkles, or inappropriate language/ images; and/ or appearance is very unkempt (0–5 points)	Wears clothes that have some rips, stains, or wrinkles; appearance is a bit unkempt (6 points)	Wears clothes that are mostly free of rips, stains, or wrinkles; appearance is mostly neat and tidy (8 points)	Wears clothes that are free of rips, stains, or wrinkles; appearance is neat and tidy (10 points)
Visuals	Poor posture that is distracting and/or difficult to see throughout due to lighting and/ or camera angle (0–5 points)	Maintains a mix of good and bad posture; may be difficult to see at times due to lighting and/or camera angle (6 points)	Maintains good posture most of the time and is positioned with mostly decent lighting and camera angle (8 points)	Maintains good posture throughout and is positioned with good lighting and camera angle (10 points)
Audio	Speaks at a rate or volume that is difficult to understand throughout (0–5 points)	Speaks at a rate or volume that is inappropriate or difficult to understand at intervals (6 points)	Speaks at an appropriate rate and volume most of the time (8 points)	Speaks at an appropriate rate and volume throughout (10 points)

	Improvement Needed	Wish You the Best, But No Thanks	Considered for a Position	Definitely Hired
Language	Uses inappropriate or offensive language (0–9 points)	Slips in and out of business appropriate language (10 points)	Uses business appropriate language most of the time (15 points)	Uses business appropriate language throughout (20 points)

Ms. Morris sends the rubric to the interviewers a week ahead of time and then meets with them for 30 minutes the day before the interviews to go over the procedures and answer any questions they have about the rubric.

Apply

Ms. Morris will be conducting the interviews over the course of two days for her 16 virtual students. Interviews are spaced 30 minutes apart, even though each interview only takes 15 minutes. The next 5 minutes are used by the interviewers to give feedback to the interviewee. The interviewee is then dismissed and the committee discusses student performance in order for Ms. Morris to arrive at an overall grade and feedback (about 5 minutes). The last 5 minutes allow a "bio break" for the interviewers. Each interviewer serves a two-hour window, interviewing four students; Ms. Morris knew it might be difficult for business leaders to block off more time than that in their schedules. The business leaders use the rubric formatively to provide feedback to students, but only Ms. Morris uses the rubric to provide a summative grade (with the business leaders' input). This helps to ensure consistency of grades between students.

Students have been told to log in to their virtual meetings at least 5 minutes before their interview time and to take that time to check their audio and cameras. Ms. Morris has previously worked with students to help them design interview appropriate backgrounds. Students with weak internet connections may keep their cameras off when speaking, but should otherwise have their cameras on. Previously, Ms. Morris showed students how to Google potential interview questions so that they could develop potential answers. During the interviews, each student is asked the following questions:

1. What is the job for which you are interviewing, and why are you interested in it?
2. What makes you the best person for this job?
3. Describe a time that you had to solve a problem by working with others. How did you solve the problem, and what did you learn from this experience.
4. Describe a time that you had an ambitious plan that did not go as expected. Describe what happened and how you handled the situation.
5. Describe your ten-year professional plan. How does this job fit in?
6. What else should we know about you that we didn't ask?

Each person on the interview committee asks two questions. For one of the two hour slots, a business leader has an emergency, so the committee is just Ms. Morris and the other business leader. In another instance, a students' power has gone out due to a storm, so Ms. Morris arranges a make-up time with that student. The shortest interview clocks in at 7 minutes, with three of the interviews going five or so minutes over the allotted 15 minutes.

Assess

After all students have completed their interviews and Ms. Morris has completed their rubrics (including both their scores and the qualitative feedback from the interview committee), she looks at the grades in aggregate and finds the following:

	Improvement Needed	Wish You the Best, But No Thanks	Considered for a Position	Definitely Hired
Quality of Answers				
Answer Completeness	1	2	7	6
Workplace Skills	1	4	6	5
Problem-Solving Skills	3	5	5	3
AVERAGE	1.67	3.67	6	4.67

	Improvement Needed	Wish You the Best, But No Thanks	Considered for a Position	Definitely Hired
	Presentation Skills			
Professional Dress	0	0	3	13
Visuals	0	0	0	16
Audio	1	1	2	12
Language	1	0	1	14
AVERAGE	*0.5*	*0.25*	*2*	*13.75*

From this, Ms. Morris can tell that she needs to continue working with students on not just presentation skills, but how to actually answer interview questions in a way that showcases their skills. Furthermore, Ms. Morris notes that all the lowest level scores came from one student, so Ms. Morris sets up a time to conference one-on-one with that student, finding out that he had been up with his sick little brother most of the night. She sets up a time to redo his interview.

Refine

Ms. Morris decides that she is going to take the questions that gave students the most trouble and have students outline answers to them and then practice with one another. Students will then use Flipgrid or a similar to record their spoken responses, which will count as another grade. She will also give students similar questions once a week and have students go into breakout rooms to practice asking each other these questions, while she visits each breakout room.

Furthermore, at the end of each interviewer's shift, Ms. Morris asked them what they did and did not like about the rubric. A few noted that while the rubric provided great specifics, it was difficult for them to quickly use; there were just too many categories and levels for them to keep in their working memory while also paying attention to student responses. Many said they felt like they were just becoming proficient with the rubric when their shift ended. For that reason, Ms. Morris decides that next time she teaches this course, she will provide business leaders with a simpler single-point rubric that uses the same categories, but only has the highest level for each. She will continue to use the more complex rubric to provide her own feedback and the actual grade for students. Here is what the single point rubric looks like:

Virtual Performance Strategies

Grows	Criteria	Glows
	Quality of Answers	
	Answer Completeness	
	Fully answers each part of each question without rambling (10 points)	
	Workplace Skills	
	Gives answers that demonstrate high levels of responsibility, integrity, and perseverance (20 points)	
	Problem-Solving Skills	
	Answers demonstrate high levels of creativity and critical thinking, and the ability to work with others to solve problems (20 points)	
	Presentation Skills	
	Professional Dress	
	Wears clothes that are free of rips, stains, or wrinkles; appearance is neat and tidy (10 points)	
	Visuals	
	Maintains good posture throughout and is positioned with good lighting and camera angle (10 points)	
	Audio	
	Speaks at an appropriate rate and volume throughout (10 points)	
	Language	
	Uses business appropriate language throughout (20 points)	

Note: There has been a lot of discussion recently about whether to include "professional dress" on rubrics such as these. It raises questions of equity, in that students with access to nicer clothes will be more likely to score higher on this category than those who do not have such access. For that reason, this rubric does not require a certain type of clothing (e.g., suit and tie) but rather that the appearance be generally tidy. Even so, an instructor should keep in mind the students in the class, and make appropriate decisions about whether to include such a category.

Ms. Morris shows this to two of the interviewers with whom she collaborates most frequently, and they agree that the single-point rubric would be much easier to use.

Virtual Performance Strategies

Professional Development Plan for This Chapter

1. Teachers gather in their thought partner groups. During this session, either there should be an outside facilitator or an appointed group facilitator to keep the group on task and on time.
2. The facilitator asks the group to share, one at a time, a written prompt for a virtual performance activity.
3. In 5 minutes: Each thought partner then shares what they feel the prompt is asking the student to do in the virtual project.
4. In 3 minutes: The teacher reflects back what they heard and shares any changes based on the feedback from the partners.
5. The protocol should be completed for the other partners in the group if they have virtual performances planned in the upcoming week or two. If there are no virtual performances planned, partners should bring previous virtual performance assignments to share and reflect on for potential revisions in the future.

Virtual Tools for This Strategy at Time of Publication

Capabilities	Google Meet	Zoom	WeVideo	Flipgrid	YouTube
Allows students to perform live	✔	✔			✔
Allows students to record and share performances	When using additional Workspace tools	Cloud storage is available at a high cost	✔	✔	✔
Allows students to provide feedback on others' performances	When live, or when using additional Workspace tools	When live		✔	✔

(*Continued*)

119

(Continued)

Capabilities	Google Meet	Zoom	WeVideo	Flipgrid	YouTube
Allows the teacher to communicate with the student during the live performance	✔	✔			✔
Allow students to view others' performances	✔	When using additional tools	✔	✔	✔
Payment level	High	High	Moderate/High	Free	Free

Quick Comparison

Google Meet is the video-conferencing platform component of *Google Workspace*, the enterprise-/organization-level of the Google tools. Teachers can use *Meet* to observe a student performance done live via a webcam, providing feedback to the student both verbally and in writing if desired. Teachers can choose to allow or not allow other students to become observers and commenters in the video session. Students can even be given permission to create their own *Meets*, even with no other attendees, and can use the recording tool to record their performance for later viewing by the teacher or peers. Recordings are stored in *Google Drives*, and can be integrated into other Google tools. Functionality on a wide range of computing devices is an advantage of *Google Meet*.

Zoom is feature comparable to *Google Meet*, and generally provides more robust security and customization features than Google's tool. The live, recorded, and peer-shared results that can be achieved in *Meet* can likewise be achieved in *Zoom*—but without the deep integration to other Google tools that schools may already have in place. On the one hand, the full Google Workspace cost can be quite high compared to *Zoom*, but on the other, *Zoom* has a very high price for what amounts to just a video-conferencing tool. Teachers and schools can experiment with some of the free tools on both platforms to begin to judge their worth.

WeVideo is an online video editor for students. Available on many kinds of devices, *WeVideo* can be used to record (and edit) performances using a webcam or using screen recording and narration. This can be particularly useful for students to demonstrate their skills with virtual manipulatives in various scenarios. Live performances are not possible, and feedback is limited to multiple students working on a single collaborative video. But WeVideo's excellent video editing tools may be ideal for complex performances where editing is actually expected in order to create a polished final product.

Flipgrid, mentioned in previous chapters, can be used by students to record performances. These recordings can be viewed and commented on by teachers and/or by other students. *Flipgrid* works on many devices, is completely free, and has simple-to-use recording tools that require little to no up-front knowledge. Creating live performances is not currently possible on Flipgrid, but crafty teachers can embed third-party live video tools such as *YouTube Live* into *Flipgrid* so that feedback on live performances can be given using the user-friendly commenting tools within the platform.

YouTube Live is perhaps the most full-featured live performance option among this group. Per its namesake, it can be used to stream student performances in real-time, and allow for live feedback from the teacher and/or other students as well. But *YouTube Live* isn't limited to live performances; recordings can be made, shared, and commented upon as well. Teachers will have to be careful with privacy, security, and channel settings. And like the other tools, *YouTube Live* is highly functional on a number of different computing platforms.

Virtual Projects

Projects are one of the best ways to increase student motivation by making learning relevant for students. Projects can range from simple to complex, and may take many different forms depending on the instructional model that is used (Smith et al., 2021). Some projects will be more difficult to complete online, especially projects in which multiple students are required to use the same materials, such as collaboratively building a robot. It can also be difficult if there are specialized materials or programs that students do not have available in their homes and it is not possible to get them the materials (for instance, some Career and Technological Education courses use 3D printers, and it is doubtful that many students have access to one of these at home). So while these kinds of projects cannot be conducted 100% virtually, there are still many other kinds of projects that can. This chapter takes a look at how to create virtual projects that are authentic and engaging, helping teachers to consider what instructional model works best with their content, whether to make projects interdisciplinary, helping students learn how to tackle projects, and the importance of addressing equity issues. It also looks at how to grade projects, including creating rubrics, giving feedback, deciding how many grades to give, and grading group work versus individual work. Lastly, this chapter will present a case study that walks readers through how a teacher might create and grade a project from beginning to end.

Creating Virtual Projects

We have worked with many teachers who are reluctant to do projects, mostly because of the time and effort these kinds of assignments require

DOI: 10.4324/9781003200093-5

from both the teacher and the students. Teachers further argue these kinds of projects do not prepare students for standardized tests, which is still the current measure of teaching effectiveness. That being said, projects prepare students for *life*, giving them the crucial skills they need beyond content knowledge, such as how to think critically and creatively, how to work in groups, and how to solve problems. And while projects generally do take more time and energy than regular classwork assignments, they also help students better understand and retain the content knowledge that they *do* learn (Chen & Yang, 2019; Johnson & Delawsky, 2013; Kanter & Konstantopoulos, 2010). Another beneficial aspect of the project is that it can be used both as an instructional model, helping students learn new information, and as an assessment to determine *what* students learned. Given that students can usually attack projects in various ways, they also imbue learning with personalization, therefore, making the projects more intriguing to students (Dynarski et al., 2008; Jones, 2008; Pane et al., 2015).

Types of Projects

There are many different ways to do projects, many of which make use of instructional models. An *instructional model* is a general approach to teaching involving a series of steps in a particular order that elicits specific student thought patterns and application of knowledge, skills, and competencies. *Project-based learning (PBL)* is a very general type of instructional model that PBLWorks.org (2021) defines as "a teaching method in which students learn by actively engaging in real-world and personally meaningful projects." Projects are typically longer assignments that result in a product, performance, or presentation, and feature high levels of student "voice and choice." In other words, students should have opportunities to make decisions about how they will complete the PBL.

Unfortunately, projects are commonly confused with classwork or homework assignments. For instance, giving students cotton balls, glue, and construction paper in order to create a flipbook of the four cloud types would be better categorized as either classwork (if done synchronously) or homework (if done asynchronously), rather than a project. Other assignments may be closer to meeting the PBL definition but still lack certain requirements. For instance, imagine an assignment in which students work in groups to make clay models of the Earth, the Sun, and the Moon, and then use stop-motion animation to demonstrate how the Moon rotates and revolves around the Earth while the Earth rotates and revolves around the Sun. Though this assignment may take longer than a single class period and students may have fun completing it, it probably does not have enough student choice to be labeled under the "PBL" umbrella.

One important aspect of all PBLs is *authenticity*. The PBL should reflect tasks and problems that take place in the real world. The PBL can be authentic to students' daily lives or to the ways in which professionals in an industry work. So, for instance, students may use mathematical computation and language arts knowledge to help a teacher decide which books to order for the classroom e-library (authentic to their lives, this project can actually be completed by students), or students may use geometrical knowledge to design a new community-center (authentic to how professionals use geometry, but not something that students can actually accomplish).

The ways in which a PBL can be designed are vast. For that reason, it can help to understand different instructional models that fall under the PBL umbrella; knowing these different models can help the teacher structure the design of the PBL itself. Being familiar with different types of PBLs can also help teachers develop ideas based on their content and students' interests. We will look at four types of PBLs: problem-based learning, performance-based learning, service learning, and inquiry-based learning. These are not the only models, but in our experience, they tend to be some of the most frequently used in the classroom.

Problem-Based Learning

Problem-based learning is frequently conflated with project-based learning, probably because they both have the same acronym (PBL). Problem-based learning, however, is actually a different instructional model that can, but does not have to, be used to develop projects. According to the Center for Teaching Innovation (2021), problem-based learning is, "a student-centered approach in which students learn about a subject by working in groups to solve an open-ended problem." These problems may have a limited scope and take a class period or less ... or they can be complex and range over longer periods of time. The most important thing about problem-based learning is that the problem is presented *before* the material, and students learn the material while working to solve the problem. Because problems are open-ended, there may be several different ways for students to actually solve the given problem, but generally, the Center for Teaching Innovation (2021) recommends that students:

- Consider the problem itself and define it in explicit terms.
- Review their own background knowledge about the topic.
- Create a plan for what else they need to know and how they will acquire that knowledge.
- Brainstorm solutions to the problem and evaluate the potential effectiveness of each.
- Implement the solution.
- Reflect on and share out their findings and conclusions.

Examples of problem-based learning prompts might be things like, "How can we mitigate the effects of erosion in our communities due to rainwater runoff?" (science), "How can a family of four meet their nutritional requirement on $100/week?" (health), or "How can we help increase the number of students reading at-grade level in a nearby elementary school?" (English). The important thing to remember about problem-based learning is that the prompt must be both a real-life problem that students have some level of agency to solve, and open-ended with many different possible solutions.

Service Learning

Service learning is a cousin to problem-based learning, in that students identify problems within their communities based on what the students are learning. Students then develop potential solutions and implement them. In service learning, there is an emphasis on working *with* the community to identify problems and implement solutions. Unlike problem-based learning, this model does not require that students receive a prompt

Virtual Projects

before instruction on the unit; teachers can teach the unit and then have students use their knowledge to complete the project. This is because the emphasis is on using what is learned in the service of others. There is also a difference between community service and service learning; *community service* does good for the community but does not necessarily seek to solve problems and may not use what students have learned. The emphasis of service learning is also on implementing actual solutions, rather than simply raising money to give to other organizations to solve the solutions. For instance, having a car wash to donate money to the Red Cross does not actually use student learning, even though it is a beneficial event. This does not mean that raising money cannot be a part of the service learning, just that it should be a means to an end rather than the desired outcome. The steps involved in a service learning project are student led and usually consist of:

1. Doing a needs assessment of the community based on the current topic;
2. Creating a plan to address the needs, including what human, capital, and other resources are needed;
3. Implementing the plan;
4. Reflecting on the effectiveness of the project to solve the identified problem; and
5. Presenting on outcomes and conclusions.

Step number 4 (Reflecting on effectiveness) is a big component in service-learning, because it teaches students to take ownership of their ability to impact their communities. One caution about service learning: There is a fine line between guiding students on their projects and just telling students what to do. A teacher using a service learning project needs to be careful to only use the least amount of support needed for students, because the main goal is teaching students that they can use what they have learned to make a difference.

Inquiry Learning

Inquiry learning also shares many attributes with problem-based learning. Unlike problem-based learning, however, inquiry projects do not necessarily require that a problem be solved. The focus is instead of students asking their own questions and then finding the answers, sometimes through reading or watching materials, but often through conducting hands-on experiments. Like the models above, the inquiry learning model is student driven, with the teacher acting as a guide for learning. One of the most frequently used lesson models for inquiry learning is the BSCS 5E Model (BSCS, 2021), which includes the following steps:

1. Engage: The teacher introduces the new topic using engaging activities that both connect the new learning to prior knowledge and pique students' curiosity to learn more about the topic. Learners may generate initial questions for study during this phase.
2. Explore: Students engage in activities (usually hands-on) that help them learn more about the concept. These may be teacher provided, or they may be student driven. In a science classroom, this phase may include actual experiments in which students generate and test hypotheses. New questions may be developed as students dig deeper into learning, and students work iteratively to generate questions and find answers.
3. Explain: Students use what they found during the Engage and Explore phases and dive deep into a particular concept in order to create an explanation about their own learning. The teacher may guide with particular lessons or explanations, but the focus is still on the student creating their own explanations based on their experiences (rather than just being told an explanation by the teacher).
4. Elaborate: Students extend their thinking, using the knowledge from the Explain phase to dive even deeper into the topic. Again, these activities may be guided by the teacher.
5. Evaluate: Students evaluate their own learning (essential); teachers may also evaluate student understanding of the topic.

One challenge to inquiry learning is that if students have never engaged in this model, they may be reluctant at first to ask their own questions. Older students, who have often been told for years their job is to memorize information handed to them from the teacher, may especially struggle at first with taking ownership of their learning. Teachers will want to gradually phase in this inquiry model, and may need to teach students how to ask questions and find their own answers.

Products and Performances

The goal of the performance or product project is to create something, whether it is a live event or a tangible object. This type of project may work to solve a problem (for instance, creating awareness of homelessness through the writing and performing a dramatic production, or inventing an app that helps students keep track of their health habits) … or the performance or product may be the goal in and of itself. For instance, a student may create a series of watercolors on plants indigenous to their community, or write and perform a pop song. Students can work together (such as four people writing a scene together and then all performing it) or independently (such as creating a sculpture). The important thing to remember if creating a project based on a product or performance is there should be high levels of student voice and choice; if the majority of the projects come out looking the same, that is, an indicator that students needed more ownership of their own learning. One example we have seen is having students create a brochure that explains the cardiopulmonary resuscitation (CPR) method and tries to persuade people to become certified in CPR. The teacher told students they were making a brochure and then gave them the template and the information that needed to be used. As a result, each brochure looked almost identical with only a few variations in font or color choices. A better way to attack this kind of project would have been to tell students they needed to create a performance or product that encouraged people to be CPR certified, therefore, giving students more avenues to creatively address the problem.

Deciding Whether to Make Projects Interdisciplinary

No matter what type of instructional model you use for your project, a question that frequently comes up is whether to combine disciplines to create the project. There are pros and cons of creating interdisciplinary projects. On one hand, typically real-world projects and problems *do* span multiple disciplines, so these types of projects are more realistic. Interdisciplinary projects also teach students to transfer their learning between subjects, helping them to make connections and retain information and skills longer. On the other hand, however, interdisciplinary projects tend to have a bigger scope than single-subject projects, meaning they often take more time and energy for students and teachers. Teachers of a certain discipline may also find they do not have the background knowledge in all the necessary subjects to effectively design an interdisciplinary project. Lastly, sometimes teachers simply want to see what students can accomplish using one or two skills that are incredibly important for the particular discipline. In other words, there is no definitive answer on whether projects should be interdisciplinary, and teachers can use their judgment based upon their content.

That being said, some of the most creative projects we have seen have been created by taking two disciplines that might not intuitively seem to "fit" and finding areas where they do overlap. For instance, one fourth-grade project that featured social studies and music as the main disciplines had students use music to analyze the history of American cultural groups. Another seventh-grade project focused on art and science by having students use their knowledge of plants to create paintings of flowers and all their parts, but in the style of various artists. One of the best ways to create these kinds of interdisciplinary projects is to find a teacher of a subject area other than yours, take out all your standards or learning objectives, and see what connections can be made. If teachers share students, then each teacher can also guide different parts of the project, and each teacher can grade their own portions (since a science teacher may not feel comfortable grading students' artistic skills).

Of course, virtual teachers may be less likely to have access to teachers in other disciplines, especially if everyone is working remotely. There are, however, many social media groups for virtual teachers. If a teacher uses a particular platform, that platform may have its own teacher groups' social media pages. Another great place to find other teachers willing to collaborate is on the Flipgrid #gridpals site, where teachers across the world can seek to collaborate with other classes. While the type of integration listed above (in which each teacher leads and grades different parts of the project), that level of integration is not necessary. Two teachers of different subjects can still work together to create a project, even though they will teach it separately, or a teacher of one subject can act more as a "consultant," giving advice based on a project mostly designed by a teacher of another subject.

Teaching Students How to Do Projects

We have met several teachers who have done projects that left a proverbial bad taste for this format of learning. Frequently, they cite projects that ended up taking too much time, students who weren't motivated to complete the project, and because of all this, the project took away time from "real content" (i.e., what would be tested on a standardized assessment). Almost all of these situations can be avoided depending on the way that the teacher designs the project. One of the key things to remember is that students have to learn *how* to do projects before they can learn *by* doing projects. There are two main things teachers should keep in mind when designing the projects: (1) students frequently do not have fully developed executive functions skills, and (2) students may need instruction on how to use technology to accomplish the (5Cs [communication, collaboration, critical thinking, creative thinking, and citizenship]).

Teaching Executive Function Skills

Have you ever forgotten a doctor's appointment? Do you find yourself annoyed when friends change their plans last minute? Have you ever said something you later regretted? Do you tend to run late? Have you ever put off writing a paper until the day before it was due? If the answer to any of these questions is "yes," then you've experienced the results of what happens when our executive function skills are not firing on all cylinders. According to the Harvard Center on the Developing Child (n.d.), executive function skills are "the mental processes that enable us to plan, focus attention, remember instructions, and juggle multiple tasks successfully." While there are several different frameworks for the various skills that can be described as "executive function skills," they generally include skills such as time management, planning and prioritization, goal-driven persistence, organization, and emotional control (Dawson & Guare, 2009). If you read that list, you realize that frequently *adults* struggle with these skills, and children and young adults are even more likely to struggle with them because the area of the brain that controls executive function, the cerebral cortex, does not finish fully developing until a person is in their mid-twenties. People also tend to be stronger in some executive function skills than others. However, *all* these skills are essential for students to complete projects.

The good news is the brain has a certain amount of malleability, and these skills can be taught (Dawson & Guare, 2009). If, however, students are not naturally skillful in a particular area, *and* they have never been taught strategies for being successful, they are likely to not do well on projects. And many students, when faced with the prospect of failing, will choose to fail on their own terms, usually without wasting the effort of trying. After all, if you've been a couch potato your whole life, what would you do if someone said you needed to run a marathon tomorrow in order to pass a class? We think it's safe to say most people would laugh and go back to watching Netflix. This is exactly what projects can feel like to students who have never done them before. That being said, if you offer the couch potato a scaffolded Couch-to-5K program over a course of several weeks, along with the support of a personal trainer, they are more likely to consider it.

For these reasons, it is crucial that teachers teach students not only the content, but *how* to do the project. The teacher needs to implement a scaffolded system to complete the project and offer continual support. If doing a project with a particular class for the first time, teachers should not assume students will know how to break up a project into parts, assign parts to group members, develop questions, research answers, keep track of their materials, or know how to manage their time. Teachers also should not assume that students who do not know how to do the following are lazy or unmotivated (though that may be how they seem). When students are "lazy," it generally means one (or all) of the following: (1) there is not enough voice and choice in the project; (2) students do not see how the project is relevant to their lives or their future goals; or (3) students have no idea how to tackle the project.

Using Project Phases and Feedback. We recommend teachers make students complete a project in phases, and during each phase, the teacher should check in with students to see the progress that has been made and provide feedback. Giving timely and helpful feedback is one of the most supportive things a teacher can do for students completing a project. A study by Koenka et al. (2019) found students who received feedback were more motivated and achieved at higher levels when compared to those who received only grades. If students are completing a project completely on their own, then frequently what will actually be graded is whether they are naturally skillful at executive function skills or whether anyone has taught them how to do projects in the past … neither of which have anything to do with what the teacher is actually teaching the students. Breaking up assignments and giving students feedback along the way also mirrors real-life; frequently employees check in with their bosses on big projects to give updates and potentially brainstorm solutions to issues.

What, then, should the phases be? Again, there are no right or wrong answers to this, but we recommend that, at a minimum, teachers check in with students at least at the beginning, middle, and end of a project. For longer projects, teachers may want to do weekly check-ins. Another method is to use the steps in the relevant instructional model. For instance, if doing a problem-based learning project, teachers may want to review and provide feedback: (1) after students first unpack and define the problem, (2) once they record their own background knowledge and determine what else they need to know, (3) after they have acquired the new knowledge, (4) after they choose a solution, (5) after the implement the solution, (6) and then after they reflect and share their findings.

This kind of feedback can be synchronous or asynchronous. Teachers can meet with individuals or groups one-on-one, in breakout rooms, or give feedback using the comments feature on Google Drive or Microsoft Office programs. Many teachers like to use an online, shared scrum chart (such as with Google Docs or Google Sheets), in which students keep track of their work in the various phases that the teacher has chosen. This allows the teacher to quickly see where individuals or groups are in the process and keeps any students from getting "lost in the mix." Groups can also link their current work so that teachers can visit their group documents and provide specific feedback. Below is an example of a scrum chart for a project in which students had to update and perform a scene from Shakespeare via Zoom.

Directions: Mark each column with a "yes" when you have completed this step, and then link your work. The teacher checks all links on Tuesdays and Fridays and provides feedback.

	Scene chosen? (Due 04/01)	Brainstorm completed? (Due 04/03)	Rough draft written? (Due 04/10)	Final draft written? (Due 04/17)	Filming done? (Due 04/23)	Editing done? (Due 04/30)
Group 1 Student A Student B Student C Student D	Yes—first scene of R&J (didst thou bite thy thumb at me)	Yes	Yes—need a conference with teacher			
Group 2 Student E Student F Student G	Yes. Hamlet talking to father's ghost	Yes	Yes. Conference completed.	Yes	Filming on Tuesday	
Group 3 Student H Student I Student J Student K	Yes— Katherine & Petruchio meet for the first time in Taming of the Shrew	Yes	Almost			

A benefit of a scrum chart like this is that, in addition to making it easy for the teacher to find all students' work and keep track of where they are in the project, it also keeps students accountable when they see where other individuals or groups are in the process of completing their own projects.

Teaching Technology and the 5Cs

We discussed the importance of teaching students how to use the required technology in Chapter 4, but using technology for projects can be even more involved, especially if students are required to use it to think critically or creatively, collaborate, or effectively communicate. Students are likely to be using more than one program to complete their projects, such as could be seen in the Shakespearean Zoom assignment. Students had to use a word processor such as Google Docs in order to write their rough draft, then using a software that allows teleconferencing and recording, such as Zoom, and lastly, use a software that allows them to edit their recordings. Teachers may also find themselves having to teach students how to use programs that help them communicate with one another. For instance, students using a shared Google Drive might need to be taught how to make copies, check revisions, alter share permissions, move documents from one folder to another, etc. We cannot assume students know these things; while they may be savvy at social media, they frequently are not used to using technology to collaboratively create things. Teachers may need to teach skills that we take for granted, such as how to leave comments, and when and how to resolve comments. For instance, it might seem obvious, but we have worked with several students (including graduate students) who look at all comments from the teacher as "suggestions," and will click the "resolve" button without actually taking the teacher's advice. We have had to literally show students how to read a comment, remind them not take it personally, and then apply the advice.

Students may also need to be taught how to collaborate over technology, especially if working in shared docs. For instance, students need to understand the protocol for going in and making changes to group work; it may not occur to them that they simply should not go in and change everything without alerting their group members. It may be necessary for teachers to give students parameters for when they can make changes without notifying their group members and discussing it with them first.

Students may also not be used to some of the more "old-fashioned" technologies if they need to reach out to members of the community to complete a project. For instance, Kate likes to tell the story of her then 10-year old, who she asked to call her cell phone and check whether her voicemail was working. He called and hung up after three rings. She reminded him to wait until voicemail came on. He called again and again hung up after three rings. "Why aren't you waiting for voicemail?" she cried. "I don't even know what voicemail is!" he yelled back in despair. He had grown up in the age of cell phones, where he would call friends and family and if they didn't answer, he hung up. They would see that he called, and call him back at their convenience. He had literally never let a phone call go to voicemail.

Similarly, this same young man needed to be taught how to send a proper email to teachers, and that using abbreviations like he uses in texting are not appropriate when sending professional communications. He did not understand how to effectively use the subject line, or he needed a greeting, or he should have a signature. Before we spoke, he literally thought email was simply a less efficient way to text. Teachers cannot assume their students understand how to use technology for effective communication, and upon finding out students do not have these skills, teachers will need to implement lessons on these "old-fashioned" methods of communication rather than marking students down and being frustrated at the students for "not trying." Remember, this is the generation that *doesn't even know what voicemail is*.

Students also need to be taught digital citizenship. Especially in a classroom where students may not have worked together in-person before, it is very important that the teacher teach students how to give one another feedback in a kind and thoughtful manner. Also, if the teacher wants students to work in groups, it is advisable to assign roles and model how each role should go about their job. If students have mainly used technology to talk to others one-on-one, they may not understand how to successfully work in an online group. Things such as when to turn on your camera, what to do if you accidentally talk over someone else (which can happen frequently with internet delays), and how to responsibly use the chat feature are all things that students may need to be taught. Students are used to scrolling through YouTube or TikTok, but may not have been taught how to evaluate sources for bias. Students also may not understand parody.

One thing we encourage teachers to do is to think about all the technology and 5C tasks that students will be required to do to complete the project. Survey students before the project on how comfortable they are and/or how much experience they have with these skills, maybe using a formative assessment tool such as Poll Everywhere or Google Forms. The teacher can then use this information to give whole group or small group lessons on how to effectively use the various technologies as needed.

A Word About Equity

It is important to always remember that students do not come from homes with the same materials resources and adult support, and it is even more important to remember this when doing virtual projects. When doing projects in a brick and mortar classroom, it is possible for the teacher to provide materials to students; this may or may not be possible in the virtual classroom. For this reason, we suggest that projects either require the use of materials that can be easily found in almost any household (e.g., toilet paper rolls, cereal boxes) or exclusively use online resources that are free to students. If projects require students to buy materials or software, then we may unintentionally be assessing students' family pocketbooks rather than student learning.

It is also important to remember that not all students have the same level of support at home. Some older students may be alone or watching younger siblings while parents work. Older students may be holding down jobs in addition to taking classes, requiring flexibility. These are reasons that it is important that the *teacher* provide any necessary training, rather than expecting parents or other family members to help students with it. Furthermore, virtual teachers should provide class time to complete the projects as much as possible, especially if group work is involved. Many students who are enrolled in virtual classes may be doing so because of the flexibility it offers; teachers cannot assume that students will have similar schedules that allow them to virtually meet outside of school time. Giving time for project work during regular class time also makes teachers more available to students, as students may not have individuals at home to help them when they work outside of regular class hours.

Grading Virtual Projects

Virtual projects can present some challenges with grading. Projects can have many parts to them, requiring teachers to make several decisions, such as:

- What parts should be graded? What parts should only receive feedback?
- What is "fair" to include in the rubric? What is not?
- Will there be one final grade, or a series of grades throughout? If the project is interdisciplinary, are the grades being split into different content areas, or will they be aggregated together?
- How can group work be graded fairly?

This section will take a look at each of these questions in turn, providing teachers with more questions to consider in order to make judgments based upon their professional opinions. We will also give some example rubrics and suggest grading procedures that can make the process easier for both teachers and students. First, we will look at the importance of good feedback. Then, we will turn to the question on what kind of rubric to create, and what categories to include. Then, we consider how to create an appropriate grading scheme, including how many separate grades to give. Lastly, we will discuss how to handle grading group work in a way that looks at the project as a whole but also takes into account individual participation in the project.

Giving Good Feedback

Grades are one method of providing feedback to students, but they are usually very general. A student who earns a B but receives no other form of feedback will not know why points were deducted or how they could have done better. Without this important feedback, it is difficult for students to improve on any future projects. If the whole point of project-based learning is just that—to learn—then it is essential that teachers give quality feedback. Furthermore, we recommend giving feedback frequently throughout the project rather than waiting until the end to give feedback. Projects generally require a series of steps, or phases, that build upon one another, and if students misunderstand early phases, they will likely not do well in later phases, either. This is, quite frankly, a waste of everyone's time ... both the student who is doing it incorrectly and the teacher who is grading it and will have to reteach what the student failed to grasp.

Teachers can give feedback synchronously or asynchronously, and we recommend a combination of both throughout the project. Synchronous feedback, in which the teacher meets with either the individual or the group, is beneficial because students can ask clarifying questions of the teacher, and the teacher can provide personalized support to students who are significantly struggling. There are two main ways to give synchronous feedback: The teacher can watch as the group or individual works in "real-time," or the teacher can review completed work and then meet with students to deliver feedback. We recommend that teachers do both. Watching students work in "real-time" can help to address misconceptions early; if groups are experiencing personality conflicts, the teacher can also help the group work through these. It is also important to review the work holistically after students complete each phase. This allows the teacher to ensure that students are completing the work correctly before allowing them to move on. Teachers should have students make any corrections before allowing students to move on to the next phase. These "end of phase" conversations can also give students the chance to ask about the next phases, therefore, helping to streamline their work and understand how the different phases fit together.

Asynchronous feedback tends to take place as teachers review work after a predetermined stopping point, whether it's the end of a phase or the end of a specific time period. For instance, a teacher might decide to review student progress each Wednesday and Friday. Teachers can use comment features on documents to give specific feedback on various elements, and then also give holistic feedback about the main things that students should work on, or things that are harder to pinpoint in work, such as overall organizational structure, tone, etc.

How the teacher chooses to give feedback should depend on the structure of the class, the project, and the needs of the students. Students who are used to doing projects may not need as much feedback (though we still recommend that teachers check students' work as they complete each phase). To help figure out when and how they will give feedback, we encourage teachers to use a chart like this one.

	During Phase	*End of Phase*
Phase:	Synchronous/Asynchronous?	Synchronous/Asynchronous?
Phase:	Synchronous/Asynchronous?	Synchronous/Asynchronous?
Phase:	Synchronous/Asynchronous?	Synchronous/Asynchronous?

Let's look at an example of how a teacher might use this chart for a project that took place during an entirely asynchronous class for 9–12 year olds. The task (entitled "Pick Your Own Path") was to write a story with multiple pathways for the reader to choose, and then put it in a Google Slides or PowerPoint presentation with working hyperlinks so that readers of the story could choose different paths and arrive at different endings. Here is the feedback plan:

	During Phase	*End of Phase*
Phase: Brainstorm and Research	Asynchronous: Instructor available to answer questions via private message	Asynchronous: Instructor leaves individual comments on the Google Doc or Word doc, and sends holistic feedback via private message. Students make necessary changes and resubmit before moving on.
Phase: Project Outline	Asynchronous: Instructor available to answer questions via private message	Asynchronous: Instructor leaves individual comments on the Google Slides presentation or PowerPoint, and sends holistic feedback via private message. Students make necessary changes and resubmit before moving on.
Phase: Writing	Asynchronous: Instructor available to answer questions via private message	Asynchronous: Instructor leaves individual comments on the Google Slides presentation or PowerPoint, and sends holistic feedback via private message. Students make necessary changes and resubmit before moving on.

Providing feedback each step of the way, and making sure that students made any necessary changes before moving on, ensured that students got to the end with quality products.

Virtual Projects

Once a teacher has decided *when* to give feedback, it's important to know *how* to give the feedback. One thing we encourage teachers to do when giving feedback to let students know what feedback is *optional to consider* and what changes noted in feedback are *required*. Do not assume students will automatically know this; we have even had grad students (teachers of all ages!) who assume that *all* feedback is optional and resubmit in papers with all comments resolved and next to no actual changes made. We also recommend the teacher tell students what is working well in addition to what can be improved (especially if this is the first time working with the student). We prefer the Glows-Grows-Next Steps method of feedback. Feedback that is framed positively can have a major impact on students. For instance, in the Pick Your Path project, one student, who was obviously reluctant to do the assignment, turned in a brainstorming sheet that made it clear that his main characters were whatever he happened to see on his desk when completing his work (e.g., a pencil as the main character, an eraser as the villain). Then, as if to prove the ridiculousness of the whole assignment, he set the story in outer space. He masterfully fulfilled every requirement by doing the absolute minimum amount of work. The instructor had two choices: scold him for not taking it seriously … or go with it. Here is the feedback that the instructor gave:

> Hi Student X,
> Thank you for submitting this! These are some of the most inventive characters I have ever seen on an assignment like this and I must admit, I laughed out loud at the idea of a character named Pencil with his mortal enemy being Eraser … and the whole thing being set in space. I can already tell that this story is going to be one of the most creative I've seen.
>
> A couple of things: You wrote a couple of words about each character. Can you add one or two sentences for each character that describe their background, their hobbies, major personality traits, etc.? Once you get to writing the rough draft, having this information already written down will help the process go more smoothly and will allow you to focus more on the plot points.
>
> Your sense of humor really came through and I am very excited to see what you come up with next. Once you add those brief descriptions, resubmit the work just so I can spotcheck, and then I'll let you know when you're good to go on to your outline.

This student did, indeed, go on to turn in one of the most creative stories the instructor had seen. He did not write paragraphs and paragraphs per slide (as did some of the other students), but every slide was finished (frequently beyond minimum expectations) and it was clear that he enjoyed how absurd he got to make the story. His parent later revealed the students was a reluctant writer, so keeping feedback positive, while still pointing out things that can be improved and what changes need to be made, was key in getting him to finish the project and meet all the requirements.

Feedback, and specifically forward feedback, is a powerful moderator in student success and an essential component in a successful learning process (Sanzo, Myran, & Caggiano, 2014). Forward feedback "provides information that students can use to adjust their performance as they work towards a learning goal" (Sanzo, Myran, & Caggiano, 2014, p. 19). Teachers who do not give specific feedback where students can understand their learning, as well as misconceptions, and make learning adjustments are not productive and could be harmful to student learning (Sanzo, Myran, & Caggiano, 2014). Effective feedback is "clear, purposeful, meaningful, and compatible with students' prior knowledge and to provide logical connections" (Hattie & Timperley, 2007).

Building Your Rubric

Another way to determine what feedback you will give is to refer back to your rubric or rubrics. While it is possible to grade projects with checklists, and it may make sense for a few projects (such as the "egg drop" project where students must create a container that will keep a raw egg from cracking when dropped from high off the ground; the egg either survives or it doesn't), the majority of work being graded will require professional judgment regarding the quality, accuracy, and clarity.

For projects, we generally recommend task-specific rubrics. Because of how projects are built, there are usually many parts that need to be graded, and it can be difficult to use a general rubric for all projects. To determine how many categories you should use for your rubric, we recommend reviewing the project, and determining the main objectives that students need to accomplish. For instance, imagine a social studies project in which a student must build the five major regions of Virginia in Minecraft to include the major landforms and resources of each region, then do a screen capture video to show the various required elements. A teacher might decide on the following elements for grading: (1) accuracy (are all the resources included in the correct regions?); (2) clarity (does the student clearly explain each region and the Minecraft elements they used to represent the landforms and the resources?); and quality (does the student show creativity in the Minecraft elements that they chose, and do those elements make sense?). Such a rubric may look something like this:

	Beginning	Emerging	Developing	Finished
Content (Accuracy)	Less than half the regions are built, and/or there are numerous inaccuracies regarding landforms and resources.	The majority of the regions are built or regions contain less than half of the landforms and resources described on the task sheet.	All five regions are built and correctly contain the majority of the landforms and resources described on the task sheet.	All five regions are built and contain all landforms and resources described on the task sheet.
Screen recording (Clarity)	The screen recording is missing, or the explanations are difficult to understand throughout the recording.	Regions are discussed but there are multiple points where the explanation of landforms and resources are unclear.	Each region is discussed and the majority of the landforms and resources are clearly explained.	Each region is discussed and the landforms and resources are clearly explained.
Creativity (Quality)	There is a lack of creativity, or depictions do not make sense even with explanation.	Some creativity in representing landforms and regions is evident and/or are frequently dependent on explanations for understanding.	Creativity in representing landforms and regions is evident, though occasionally may require explanation.	Creativity in representing landforms and regions is highly evident, while also making sense without requiring an explanation.

The words that are chosen to represent the various levels of proficiency should also reflect the underlying goal of the project. In this Minecraft rubric, the levels names of Beginning, Emerging, Developing, and Finished represent the idea that students all start at the Beginning Level, and then gradually move up each level as they work. The idea is that success is attainable and the result of perseverance rather than natural ability. This makes sense for a long-term product-based project in which students are slowly building a world.

This type of rubric works well in a project that can be successfully completed given the appropriate amount of effort, but it may not work for other learning designs, such as problem-based learning or service learning. For instance, in some problem-based projects, the solution may not actually be implementable (imagine a science project in which students are meant to devise solutions to stop the current honeybee shortage around the world). In these cases, the teacher might use a category that describes feasibility rather than actual success. Such a category may look something like this:

	Needs Improvement	*Good*	*Excellent*
Feasibility and Probability of Success	The solution is one that meets one or none of the following conditions: could be implemented with available resources; takes human nature into consideration; and has a high probability of success.	The solution is one that meets two of the following conditions: could be implemented with available resources; takes human nature into consideration; and has a high probability of success.	The solution is one that meets all three of the following conditions: could be implemented with available resources; takes human nature into consideration; and has a high probability of success.

In other cases, students may implement solutions to problems, and those solutions may not work. When this happens, the teacher needs to consider the scope of the project and whether the true goal is creating a solution or the learning that comes with the solution. In service-learning, for example, students in a government class may decide to tackle an issue such as getting more people in their community registered to vote. Students will work with the teacher online to develop the project, but then will implement the actual solutions in real life, bringing back artifacts to describe how the project went. Students may even work with the virtual teacher to set goals regarding what success should "look" like (e.g., increase the number of registered voters in the county by 5% of the current number). Suppose a student devises a robust plan, conducts in-depth research, talks to all the right people, spends hours going door-to-door and engaging in other "get-out-the-vote" campaigns ... and the number of registered voters only goes by 2%. Should this be considered a failure? We would argue that frequently, failure is but a stop on the way to eventual success. In the real world, a person with this kind of goal would take everything they learned and then implement an even better campaign the next year. Should a student who learned a great deal, became a better citizen, and helped enfranchise others receive a lowered grade? For these reasons, we believe that teachers need to think deeply about projects such as these, and what it truly means to be "successful" in a class. We suggest that the rubric defines success as the amount of work and learning that took place, or, if success must be defined by meeting goals, that those goals be a small part of the grade when compared to the learning and work.

Creating Your Grading Scheme

Each phase in a project usually builds on the phase before it, and we recommend that teachers grade each phase as students complete it. This serves multiple purposes: (1) it saves the teacher from having to do a ton of grading at the end of the project; (2) students receive feedback throughout the process and are not surprised by any grades at the end; and (3) the teacher can require students to revise and resubmit phases of the project so that subsequent phases are not unduly influenced by earlier phases that were not done to required standards.

The question then becomes, should the entire project be worth one grade, or should it be worth multiple? The answer, of course, is that it depends. For smaller projects that are only a fraction of the overall curriculum, we recommend a single grade with a single rubric, though teachers may grade different parts of the rubric as students complete the project. In some classes, however, the project itself is the main point of the course. Consider an art course in which the goal is to develop a portfolio; it makes sense for each part to be a separate grade.

Interdisciplinary projects provide another grading challenge: Should the grades be applied to separate courses, or all to the same course? Imagine a mathematics project in which students must create a children's book that explains the process of long division. The rubric will most likely include sections to grade the writing and the presentation/artwork. We recommend splitting the grade into different subjects, as makes sense, if the amount of work required in a particular subject is substantial enough to warrant a separate grade *and* either of the following conditions are met: (1) The teacher teaches the students in both subject areas; or (2) The teacher has worked with the teacher of the other subject areas to create the project, *and* they share the same students. If splitting the grades into different subject areas, teachers should take into account how much work was required in each discipline, and use that to determine the weight of the project on the final grade.

Another question that we are frequently asked pertains to group work—specifically, whether to give group or individual grades. The rationale for group grades, of course, is that is frequently how real life works; city planners don't earn individual grades for the parts of the cities they design. On the other hand, in a learning situation it does make sense to grade individuals on their separate amounts of effort. Who has not been stuck in a group project in which one or two people do the majority of the work while everyone else in the group coasts, and then suffered the indignity of everyone getting the same grade? There are a few ways to prevent this:

- The teacher should give students work time during synchronous classes, and rotate through breakout rooms to observe group interactions. True, this does not stop some students from participating when they see the teacher and then going back to scrolling social media as soon as the teacher leaves, but it at least reflects the idea that the teacher cares whether everyone is pulling their own weight.
- The teacher can use programs that track who does what, such as the Google docs revisions feature. Teachers can also have students create group scrum charts that say who completes which part of the project.

- The teacher can provide individual grades by having students do personal reflections on the work they contributed, what worked well, what changes they would make if doing the project again, etc. If the teacher is afraid of students faking their way through a written reflection, the teacher can also do individual conferences with students, which are harder for students to fake.

Case Study

Identify

Prisha Patel teaches a senior level English class on World Literature as a part of her public school system. All students in the program are issued Chromebooks. As an end-of-unit project, she has students work individually to choose one of the stories they read to create an "alternate ending" short video. These videos should be between 3 and 5 minutes long, incorporate several details, including all main characters and at least half of the most important minor characters, from the original work, and be either created through live-acting, drawings (stick figures are fine) or claymation. The purpose of the project is to demonstrate students' comprehension of the works, as well as their abilities to think analytically and creatively to create an alternative ending that would make sense and follow the tone of the original story. Prisha creates a rubric (seen in the Assess phase) to give to students before the project so that they can self-assess as they work.

Plan

After doing a review of free video editing programs, Prisha decides to use the free version of WeVideo for her students. Although the free version only allows for up to 5 minutes of video per month and adds a watermark to the video, it has the most tools for the functionality that she needs. Therefore, the month before the project, Prisha has her students create reenactments of a different short story, choosing at that time whether they want to do live acting, drawings, or claymation. Prisha tells her students that they will need to pay attention because they will have a larger project using the same skills in a month. She invites students to come to small groups at different times based upon their modality preference, and does short lessons on the most important things to know about working with that medium in WeVideo. She records these short tutorials so that students can refer back to them later if they have questions. She also invites students to help sessions for their various mediums. Students update a scrum chart every Monday and Thursday to explain where they are in their projects, taking pics as they go for "quick check" grades. These "pre-project" videos count as a classwork grade so that students can concentrate more on the feedback that Prisha gives rather than worrying about the grade. Students are allowed to revise and resubmit their videos up to three times based on feedback, and all students score a 90 or higher.

Apply

Prisha implements the actual project the next month. For three classes beforehand, she shows students an alternative ending to a popular movie (one that she knows that all students have seen by using a Google forms survey) and students analyze why the alternative ending was not used in the theatrical cut and how well it captured the tone of the rest of the movie. She then explains the project to students and has them review the rubric. They are given time to ask any questions. Prisha shows students the rubric for the project, and has them practice using it on some sample alternative ending videos that she made on different stories from the previous course students took. She has students practice grading these sample projects, and then she explains how she would have graded each project and why.

	Novice	*Apprentice*	*Proficient*	*Master*
Plot Elements (30 points)	The ending demonstrates an inadequate understanding of characters, setting, and/or events and/or contains major misconceptions. *(0–17 points)*	The ending demonstrates a limited understanding of characters, setting, and events; may contain minor misconceptions. *(18–22 points)*	The ending demonstrates an adequate understanding of characters, setting, and events. *(24–27 points)*	The ending demonstrates an adept understanding of characters, setting, and events. *(28–30 points)*

(Continued)

Virtual Projects

(Continued)

	Novice	Apprentice	Proficient	Master
Tone (30 points)	Tone is vastly different from the original work. *(0–17 points)*	Tone is uneven, aligned with original work at times and not at others. *(18–22 points)*	Tone is mostly aligned with the original work, with very minor variations. *(24–27 points)*	Tone is strongly aligned with the original work, as if written by the author him/her/themself. *(28–30 points)*
Creativity (30 points)	The alternative ending is unclear or very close to the original. *(0–17 points)*	The alternative ending feels somewhat forced and may not be fully satisfying. *(18–22 points)*	The alternative ending is a somewhat predictable but still satisfying take on the original. *(24–27 points)*	The alternate ending is an innovative take on the original that adds further depth to the original work, while still flowing seamlessly with what came before it. *(28–30 points)*
Reflection and Analysis (10 points)	Reflection demonstrates lack of understanding of the original work and/or presents an inadequate analysis of strengths and weaknesses of the finished student project. *(0–4 points)*	Reflection demonstrates minimal understanding of the original work and/or presents a minimal analysis of strengths and weaknesses of the finished student project. *(5–6 points)*	Reflection demonstrates an adequate understanding of the original work through analysis of strengths and weaknesses of the finished student product. *(7–8 points)*	Reflection demonstrates a deep connection to the original work through analysis of strengths and weaknesses of the finished student product. *(9–10 points)*

She then gives them the following due dates, and explains that after each due date, they will be given feedback that should be taken into consideration before turning in the next portion.

Week	Task	Percentage of Final Grade
Week 1	Story chosen	–
Week 2	Alternative outline completed	Classwork grade
Week 3	Storyboarding/script completed	Classwork grade
Week 4	Rough draft of project	–
Week 5	Final editing/submission of project	Final draft: 90%
Week 6	Revisions and resubmissions (if necessary), final reflections	Final reflection: 10%

Prisha reminds students that while her expectation is that students turn in quality projects in Week 5, any students who score lower than a 90% will be able to revise and resubmit in order to bring up their grades.

Assess

After the final submissions by all students, Prisha collects data on how the 16 students in her class scored overall:

	Novice	Apprentice	Proficient	Master
Plot Elements (30 points)	0 students	1 student	10 students	5 students
Tone (30 points)	0 students	4 students	6 students	6 students
Creativity (30 points)	2 students	4 students	8 students	2 students
Reflection and Analysis (10 points)	0 students	2 students	10 students	4 students

Prisha sees that students struggled most with the creative thinking part of the assignment. In talking to the students afterward, many of them express that they had never been required to do more than show evidence of comprehension and analysis; writing in the style of the author was something

Virtual Projects

very new to them. Students did not feel that the technology part was overly taxing, but they did wish that, in addition to getting feedback from Ms. Patel, they could have also either worked in small groups or at least had time to brainstorm with peers.

Refine

Prisha considers the students' suggestion to work in groups. While she still thinks it's important to have students work independently on the project, in order to assess each students' understanding and creative thinking, she decides that it makes sense to offer students more opportunities throughout the course to think creatively about literature, in addition to analyzing it. For that reason, she decides that she will implement "Free Write Fridays," in which a portion of the class will be devoted to students doing a creative writing assignment based on the current work(s) they are studying. Sometimes students will work in small groups and sometimes they will work independently, and they will be able to review each other's work and provide feedback, in addition to Prisha herself providing feedback. She begins the "Free Write Fridays" with her students and at the end of the semester, allows students a chance to do an additional alternative ending project as extra credit. Interestingly, she has two students with stellar grades ask to complete the extra credit project; they would like her feedback because they want to create a YouTube channel in which they post more videos of alternative endings for classic stories.

Professional Development Plan for This Chapter

This plan is suggested as a debrief after a virtual project as a way for teachers to unpack the lesson and reflect on their students' experiences through the lens of their thought partners.

1. The lesson—or most likely lessons—for the virtual project should be shared with the thought partners in advance of the student work review and thought partners should read through the lesson plans prior to the student work review process.

2. The teacher should house the student products in an easily accessible virtual location for thought partners to explore. This most likely will be the same platform the students loaded their work.
3. Thought partners will use the rubric used by the teacher for the virtual project and provided to students to review the student work. While not grading each project, thought partners should reflect on the student work and holistically assess if the students were meeting the expectations set forth in the lessons and on the rubric.
4. For 10 minutes: The teacher team, upon completion of reviewing the work (which can be done asynchronously) rotates and shares out "wonderings" about the student work related to the lessons and the rubric. "I wonder when the student did this, if they were applying x concept." The presenting teacher records the wonderings.
5. For 5 minutes: The presenting teacher discusses the comments and wonderings and reflects on those in relation to their experiences with the lesson and projects.
6. A total of 2 minutes on each thought partner: Each thought partner then reflects on how the student products affect the way they think about their own work developing and facilitating virtual projects.

Virtual Tools for This Strategy at Time of Publication

This chapter has already discussed a number of virtual tools to support your project-based learning journey. Also, because the technology needs can vary drastically from project to project, rather than comparing tools, this section will consider different tools that can be used during different phases of PBL. Note that while we may sort the tools into particular phases, the tools themselves can frequently be used in more than one phase.

Brainstorming Tools

Brainstorming tools can be as easy as a shared Google doc, but teachers might also want something that has more flexibility. *Padlet*, which is like a virtual sticky note software with more functionality than actual sticky notes, is a great way to let students type responses, respond to each other, and even sort the stickies. Let's say that you need a quick and easy way to track your students' team brainstorming of their approach to solving a local waterfowl sickness problem you've given them. The teacher can create a *Padlet* or let students create their own, and then teach students the various layouts and how to respond to and sort stickies. *Coggle* is another great tool for creating mind maps; it's also free and relatively intuitive to learn and use. *Lucidchart* can also allow students to create graphic organizers, and has more functionality than *Coggle*, so it might require more instruction from the teacher, and there are a limited number of organizers that students can create for free. In another example, imagine students in the early stages of their service learning project to improve the lives of young single parents in their neighborhood. When students need a way to share challenges that they've observed, the teacher can have them do a quick *Backchannel Chat* to get everything on the table and then narrow down how they might help.

Feedback and Self-Monitoring

Frequently, teachers need to be able to give feedback to students as they work on their projects. Using the comment feature in Google or Microsoft suites is one of the easiest ways to do this. In *Flipgrid*, students can record video updates and the teacher can use the rubric feature to provide quick feedback, or students can give each other glows and grows feedback. Similarly, in a project in which students need to turn in their written business plans to revitalize their downtown storefront area, but the teacher don't have time to meticulously review every aspect of every project, students can use *PeerGrade* once the teacher has taught them how to give constructive, rubric-based feedback that you can monitor. Teachers can also use *Google Classroom* or *Schoology* to create a self-monitoring rubric and then push out a copy to each student, rather than having to manually make individual files. The teacher then has all the rubrics in one easy place where students can turn them in during different phases of the project. If students have questions, the teacher can use *Zoom* or *Google Meet* to run communal Q&A sessions, or have private chats with students.

Design Tools

Projects frequently require students to create products, and in the virtual classroom, these are frequently virtual products. To have students create models, such as in a project where students will design and "build" a brick-and-mortar school that has features for more flexible learning, students can use products such as in *Minecraft Education* or *Tinkercad*. There is also a Chrome add-on called *Lego Builder* that allows students to build with virtual legos and then publish their designs. For projects that require graphic designs, one of our favorite products is *Canva*, which has access to a plethora of design templates and free graphics, and also features a *Canva for Education* package with an incredibly robust library of photos, clip art, and more. If students need to create videos, Screencastify is a good solution for screen recording, and WeVideo is an easy tool if students have access to Chrome browsers. If students use Macs, iMovie is also a relatively easy tool for them to learn.

Presentation Tools

Many projects end with students presenting their work in some fashion, which often requires both a presentation software and an online video platform. The most popular presentation softwares are *Google Slides* and *Microsoft PowerPoint*, though Mac users will also have access to *Keynote*. *Prezi* is a free web-based presentation software that functions as a giant whiteboard and allows the presenter to "zoom" from one section to another. *Canva* also allows users to make presentations, and while *Haiku Deck* only allows a limited number of slide decks with their free version, they have a simple, intuitive interface with high quality graphics and fonts. To have students present, teachers can use software such as *Google Meet* or *Zoom*, or can reach even wider audiences with live streaming services from *YouTube*, *Facebook*, or *Twitter*.

Summary

While we have listed some of our favorite tools for projects here, one of the best things that a teacher can do is simply type the functionality that is needed into your favorite search engine, and compare the results. Sometimes, a teacher may not know the correct search terms, so it can take a bit of digging to figure out the correct terms. For instance, if you want students to be able to add music to their videos, your search terms would actually be "multiple tracks" and "overlay." We also caution teachers to be wary of products that offer limited free editions; they can be useful but may only be able to be used a handful of times. The benefit of robust, free software is that teachers only have to teach students how to use the features once, and the students can concentrate on the content of their projects rather than trying to balance learning new material while learning new technologies.

References

BSCS 5E Instructional Model. (2021). BSCS Science Learning. Retrieved March 31, 2021. https://bscs.org/bscs-5e-instructional-model/https://bscs.org/bscs-5e-instructional-model/

Center for Teaching Innovation. (2021). Problem-based learning. Retrieved July 19, 2021. https://teaching.cornell.edu/teaching-resources/engaging-students/problem-based-learning

Chen, C. H., & Yang, Y. C. (2019). Revisiting the effects of project-based learning on students' academic achievement: A meta-analysis investigating moderators. *Educational Research Review, 26*, 71–81.

Dawson, P., & Guare, R. (2009). *Smart but scattered: The revolutionary "executive skills" approach to helping kids reach their potential.* Guilford Press.

Dynarski, M., Clarke, L., Cobb, B., Finn, J., Rumberger, R., & Smink, J. (2008). *Dropout prevention: A practice guide (NCEE 2008-4025).* Washington, DC: National Center for Education Evaluation and Regional Assistance, Institute of Education Sciences, U.S. Department of Education.

Harvard Center of the Developing Child (n.d.). Executive Function & Self-Regulation. Retrieved July 19, 2021. https://developingchild.harvard.edu/science/key-concepts/executive-function/#:~:text=Executive%20function%20and%20self%2Dregulation,and%20juggle%20multiple%20tasks%20successfully

Hattie, J., & Timperley, H. (2007). The power of feedback. *Review of Educational Research, 77*(1), 81–112.

Johnson, C. S., & Delawsky, S. (2013). Project-based learning and student engagement. *Academic Research International, 4*(4), 560.

Jones, R. D. (2008). Strengthening student engagement. *International Center for Leadership in Education, 1,* 10.

Kanter, D. E., & Konstantopoulos, S. (2010). The impact of a project-based science curriculum on minority student achievement, attitudes, and careers: The effects of teacher content and pedagogical content knowledge and inquiry-based practices. *Science Education, 94*(5), 855–887.

Koenka, A. C., Linnenbrink-Garcia, L., Moshontz, H., Atkinson, K. M., Sanchez, C. E., Cooper, H. (2019). A meta-analysis on the impact of grades and comments on academic motivation and achievement: A case for written feedback. *Educational Psychology.* DOI: 10.1080/01443410.2019.1659939

Pane, J. F., Steiner, E. D., Baird, M. D., & Hamilton, L. S. (2015). *Continued progress: Promising evidence on personalized learning.* Rand Corporation.

PBLWorks.org (2021). What is PBL? Retrieved July 19, 2021. https://www.pblworks.org/what-is-pbl#:~:text=Project%20Based%20Learning%20(PBL)%20is,world%20and%20personally%20meaningful%20projects

Sanzo, K. L., Myran, S., & Caggiano, J. (2014). *Formative assessment leadership: Identify, plan, apply, assess, refine.* Routledge.

Smith, J., Maxlow, K. W., Caggiano, J., & Sanzo, K. L. (2021). *Look, listen, learn, lead: A district-wide systems approach to teaching and learning in preK-12.* Information Age Publication.

For Product Safety Concerns and Information please contact our EU
representative GPSR@taylorandfrancis.com
Taylor & Francis Verlag GmbH, Kaufingerstraße 24, 80331 München, Germany

www.ingramcontent.com/pod-product-compliance
Lightning Source LLC
Chambersburg PA
CBHW051526230426
43668CB00012B/1758